Danny,
God Bless You—
Shirlie
Zouella

Praise for
Levitation's View

Thank you, sincerely, for forwarding a copy of your inspiring book, *Levitation's View*. I appreciate it.

Your willingness to share life's lessons with others will help many.

Dr. Myles Brand
President
The National Collegiate Athletic Association

This is a beautiful, powerful and important story. Your readers will be inspired and enriched.

Augustus A. White, III, M.D., Ph.D.
Orthopaedic Surgeon-in-Chief, Emeritus
Beth Israel Hospital
Professor of Orthopaedics
Harvard Medical School
Boston, Massachusetts

Our backgrounds differ as much as the color of our skin. Willie's God given talents were as a superstar in basketball, defying gravity. Mine was as a professional race car driver, traveling at speeds over 200 mph. We both had the same boss but He took us through different trials and tribulations on our road to salvation. We both accepted our Lord's gift at different stages of our lives with the same result: Jesus Christ forgave us for our many sins and gave us love and eternal salvation. Willie's lessons and experiences through his life (leading up to becoming a man of God) have helped inspire me to spread the word of God's forgiveness to others and discover the glory of eternal life through our Lord Jesus Christ.

This book is a must read for Christians and non-Christians alike.

Jerry Grant
First race car driver to exceed 200 mph
Irvine, California

Levitation's View

Lessons Voiced from an Extraordinary Journey

Volume II

The Wooden Years

Willie Naulls

Library of Congress Cataloging-in-Publication Data

Naulls, Willie
Levitation's View: Lessons Voiced from an Extraordinary Journey – Volume II: The Wooden Years

ISBN 0-9763709-1-3

1. Naulls, William D. (Willie)
2. Basketball – Biography
3. Athletics – Philosophy
4. Religion
5. Conduct of Life

Except as noted, Scriptural references use the New International Version of the Holy Bible.

Cover and interior design by Dr. Anne Van de Water Naulls

Cover cartoon figure by Karl Hubenthal, *The Los Angeles Examiner*, 9 March 1956.
Photograph of Willie Naulls on back cover of book and rear inside flap of dust cover by Peter A. Robertson, Father & Daughter Photography, 2001.
Photographs of UCLA Basketball are provided through permission and courtesy of ASUCLA and UCLA Sports Information.

Published by Willie Naulls Ministries
Post Office Box 7477
Laguna Niguel, California 92677-2714
willie@willienaulls.org • www.willienaulls.org

Manufactured in the United States of America
International Standard Book Number:
0-9763709-1-3

Dedicated to the Ones I love

I am thankful to God for this entire expression.

For my wife

Dr. Anne Van de Water Naulls

who is "my found Good Thing" of Proverbs' Truth.

Her loyalty and her love of God and honoring of His
Commandments taught to us by Jesus Christ
are a constant reminder to me that
God really does love me and He really does
honor His Word above all His Name.

To God be the Glory, forever and ever.

Thank you, Anne

I love you as Christ loves our Christian family.

Willie

Coach Wooden inspired in a fellow "Dog" the zeal
to mirror his passion for teaching excellence.
Dr. Bob Archer (UCLA '56-'59) developed in the
UCLA Dog Pound spirit of preparing himself to give
his best. Through sharing his knowledge with
students at Harvard Westlake School, he inspired one
of his most gifted, my daughter Malaika, to prepare for
the day that her father would impose upon her to use
what she had learned from Dr. Archer to edit this book.

Thank you, Malaika. I love you dearly.

Dad

Table of Contents

Foreword

Writing down the foundational Lessons for living that my mother and others taught me is the passion and sensed duty of my lifetime, all consuming and purposeful. I have prayed for guidance to share my story in a way that will inspire others to introspectively work out their God-created purpose. I pray this book will inspire each reader to embrace the question "Who Am I?". Unpacking my stored experiences, sharing the impact my mentors and teachers have had on me, whether positive or negative, and evaluating my contravened trek is an exhilarating opportunity to share with those searching for examples of people who have survived to prosper against great odds.

During my first nine years of life in segregated Dallas, Texas, in the 1930s and early '40s, I learned the importance of developing a strong work ethic from my mother's Biblical teachings. Teachers and coaches in the predominantly White San Pedro, California, school system rewarded my efforts as I continued to mature. I lived the acculturation of American color norms and mores at UCLA and through professional basketball under the integrating force of two coaching legends, UCLA's John Wooden and the Boston Celtics' Red Auerbach. From overt to covert, Blacks and Whites shadow-boxed toward gradually releasing selfishly sustained goals for posterity. God used His talent in me as an entrée into cross-cultural growth. I was a combatant immersed in the greater war to supersede the COLOR RACE. This faith declaration has been my venture beyond "seeing to believe" to "believing to see."

Through the 1960s, my generation had the greatest opportunity to impact open and fair competition for the first time. Physical success and exposure in sports opened up academic environments and exposed young people covered with Black skin for the first time to what was reputed to be the best academic instruction, facilities and cross-cultural contacts available.

From the 1970s, entrepreneurs tap danced around the issue of Race and Skin Color until competition to make money through winning forced the sage to the battle's inevitable conclusion: True evaluation of a man or woman is first individual, judging his or her character, talents and performance. The truth surfaced that it is counterproductive to competitive enterprise to ever separate people into the categories of Black and White.

As my life began in poverty and oppression in the ghetto of Dallas, it improved through the freedom of opportunity to work and develop spiritually, mentally and physically in my new integrated community of San Pedro (**WONDER YEARS**), advanced through the environment of open competition at UCLA (**WOODEN YEARS**) which continued into the NBA and Business World (**WORLD YEARS**), was transformed into a new birth when I committed my life to serving in the ministry of Jesus Christ (**WORD YEARS**), and has evolved into a maturing work together with God to inspire youth to work at developing the gifts and talents they were given at birth (**WITNESS YEARS**).

In retrospect, I was never embraced by the "homeboys" because I did not grow up on the East Side of Los Angeles, under the influence of the two predominantly African American high schools. Instead, I grew up in the governmental projects of San Pedro, where the vast majority of the residents of the town were White. I represent the very few African Americans from the period before Brown v. Board of Education who, at a young age, were thrust out of an all Black world into an all White world – and the fewer still who have survived to prosper. I believe that professional football Hall of Famer Jim Brown, Olympic Decathlon Champion Rafer Johnson and Harvard Medical School Professor of Orthopaedics and Orthopaedic Surgeon-in-Chief Emeritus of Beth Israel Deaconess Medical Center Augustus A. White, M.D., Ph.D., had similar histories. Because my parents sought a different route for me, I walked the tight rope of two worlds, Black and White, constantly striving to prove my abilities and worth. I benefited from being exposed to the "better" public schools and teachers in socio-economically privileged communities where parents demand that their children be presented with the best opportunities.

A first-team All-City performer in baseball and basketball in high school, I went on to earn All-America honors under Coach John Wooden at UCLA. As a member of the NBA's New York Knicks, I was honored to be the first African American team captain in integrated professional sports while earning four All-Star berths. I ended my ten year professional career as a three-time World Champion with the Boston Celtics who introduced the first all African American starting team in the history of integrated professional sports, under Coach Red Auerbach. After retiring, I launched an entrepreneurial career, developing several enterprises including take-out restaurants; a shopping center; companies specializing in professional contract negotiation and financial management, executive search, executive gifts, and residential and commercial real estate development; a bank; a thrift and loan company; an automobile dealership; and a non-profit youth training and development organization.

In the midst of my entrepreneurial pursuits, I experienced an epiphany with God Almighty. He called me to ministry, speaking forth this command:

"Get out of business and better prepare yourself to minister My Word and tell people what great things I have done in your life."

That awesome experience became the motivating moment for me to explore my Purpose here on earth. Following years of individual study and formal training, I founded a Christian based missionary ministry (Willie Naulls Ministries), the non-denominational Church of Common Ground and, most recently, Rising Stars Sports Ministry, which focuses on better preparing young people of all races through spiritual, academic and athletic leadership training and development with the result of maturing them to live in God's purpose as they prosper to serve others.

I am married to UCLA School of Medicine graduate Dr. Anne Van de Water Naulls. Our four children include Lisa, a professional singer and graduate of Stanford University and the UCLA Graduate School of Music; Shannon, a UCLA educated computer professional who is married with two children; Jonah, a former UCLA student, currently in the entertainment industry; and Malaika, a University of Florida graduate in Advertising and Business Management, also in the entertainment industry. Anne put her medical career on hold to be wife and mother indeed and available to our children as we stressed their educational, personal and spiritual growth.

For many years I avoided the subject of writing or even talking about my family. I questioned what benefit would accrue to my children by writing down the truth about their heritage. In an attempt to promote a false image of superiority, many families cover up what they perceive to be ungodly character in their parents and relatives. Children are the focus of the ministry of which God gave me His charge. He said, ". . . tell people what great things I have done in your life." One of the many things God has done in my life is encourage me to reflect upon the fact that His grace and peace have always been multiplied to me through His love of my mother's commitment to faith in His Word. God posed His question to me: Who is your mother, your father, your brother or sister? The sting of not knowing the history of my seed – my grandparents and where they came from and where they went – was lessened and even removed through the knowledge that I have a Heavenly Father who loves me. He loved me so much that He gave His Only Begotten Son for my rebirth into His family. By grace through faith in His Son, Jesus Christ, I now know that covering up the truth about a parent's abuse of the authority given him or her in the lives of their children is agreeing with lies. We are cautioned that "happy is the man who does not condemn himself by what he approves" (Romans 14:22b).

Only after God called me to ministry with specific instructions did I get a hint that a retrospective of my life's experiences could be an encouragement to others. I have mentioned in various public expressions that, when I was newly called to ministry, Pastor Jack Hayford encouraged me, prophetically I believe, to write down what God would give me to say. He said to pray about publishing a monthly ministry newsletter, which I did for two years. That experience awakened in me a desire to put down on paper God's grace in my life, and that zeal lives on in me through this book. Mom taught me that the good fruit of a Lesson learned is to be shared with others.

Levitation's View is given by the Spirit of God, to eagerly hover over each heart inspired to read its pages. He anticipates belief to inspire a confession – a declaration to do it God's Way.

My clear and present duty is upon me to write down my experiences, especially as a work to glorify God. I pray that my life story in prose and poetry will motivate those around me of all races to work at becoming the full measure of whom God created them individually to be.

I must remind myself and all who will read this second volume that I am attempting to accurately record the thoughts and reactions of a 17- to 21-year-old Black skinned man who was thrust upon the crest of the wave of integrating UCLA and Westwood and, for the first time in my life, meeting other Black people from a variety of geographical locations who were surfing in the same battle. The difficulty in this task is remembering that, in my insecurity and immaturity, I was surviving daily what I perceived to be life threatening circumstances. After all, I am more than physical and what the world saw me to be. Spirit with a soul is the life in me. Suffocating to express, trusting anyone was my test. I was learning to compete against myself alone to be my best. Not a Black skin versus a White skin fight as some leaders saw it to be, but soul to another, lamenting to be free.

Now I lay me down to sleep
yearning to express my soul does weep
In the depths of my heart I did keep
hurts overflowing – began to seep
Then one morning soon thereafter
so Empowered – my own book crafter

From deep within the darkness
of the land of my birth
came God's Light to guide me
through Mom's Lessons' Worth

Bettie Arlene Naulls

Mom's Lessons

William:

Obedience to God is required
Judgment by skin color is not of Him
inspired
Know right from wrong – and just do it
Do good and not evil; be strong – pursue it
Your actions are no better than anyone can
see
and nobody is better than you can be
so don't let what's around to see
entice you to become whom God didn't
create you to be
Use your mind to stand against wrong's
wooing
Think before you act in unwise doing
Don't be ashamed to say, "I don't know"
Wisdom is summoned when your mind
wants to grow
Tell me when evil does approach
to violate my teaching, your soul to broach,
going beyond the boundary of appropriate
action
to violate your person for their satisfaction
Care for yourself and your personal
hygiene
live by the Standard of our Lord Supreme
Study in school; observe the Word of
Faith's test
Compete with yourself alone to be God's
Best

The Wooden Years

Coach Wooden's Dog Pounders gather at the UCLA Chancellor's Residence to celebrate Coach's 75th Birthday

Who Flushed the Dogs Out?
This Dog's Retrospective on the
Influence of the Wooden Years

A sudden freshness,
development, or growth;
the experience of freshman warriors
as they labor to bring their talent forth
Infused with the Master's gift
and washed of the teacher's proclamation
every new recruit is stripped in the process
of their high school "me and my game"
     reputation
The maturity in their growth pattern
is exposed through fundamentals' repetition
inspiring each to become his or her best
Flushing the Dogs Out through Success's
     Fruition

The conclusive and beneficial effect of a coach
should be to flush out the maximum expression of
each player's God given talent.

People around the country are more impressed
to know me when they discover that I am an
athletic disciple of John Wooden. "What kind of
man is he? Is he as good as advertised?" My
relationship with Coach never broached his inner
man's convictions. He never sought my wise
counsel about anything. What in the world could
Coach John Wooden ask of me that would benefit
him? Obviously he didn't need to know me better to
win basketball games. But my mom and Coach

taught a valuable **Lesson** about attitude:

Coach: "It's what you learn after you know
it all that counts."

Mom: "It's what you learn after you *think*
you know it all that counts."

Coaches can be thought of as dog trainers. A trainer's reward to a good dog is a bone. In basketball terms, a bone means playing time. Of course there are dogs and then there are DOGS. They all have to be trained to be obedient to do what their masters train them up to perform: Birding, Guarding, Fetching, Herding or Catching . . . . Coach Wooden's teaching "flushed out" of his dogs "a feeling of animation or exhilaration, a sudden freshness, development and growth." In that sense, we were the DOGS whom Coach "flushed out" during our eligibility and acceptance into his world.

The word "dog" – in contrast to its previous negative connotation when referring to humans – is used as an affectionate term of identification between some young people today. That connotation is my intent herein. Potential confusion can be defused when one considers that all dogs, whether four-legged or two-legged, need training.

"Pedigree" is a word to indicate ancestry, lineage, a purebred animal. In the Bruin Pound, the rules of Pedigree were clearly established by Coach John Wooden. Hear ye, hear ye!

Giving your best, his players agree,
was the surefire way to Coach Wooden's
Pedigree.

So any Bruin dog could become a Bruin DOG of

Pedigree upon graduation simply by giving his all, no matter how well he had been fed with playing time. No one could obtain Pedigree status without graduation. After all is said and done, each of us dogs was a student first in Coach's eyes.

Coach Wooden blew his whistle and pointed out directions to his players. He began his dog training with teaching the fundamentals of the proper donning of socks and shoes and proceeded methodically up to the crown of proper grooming. The reward for obedience to those rules was the opportunity to contest for a bone. He had all of the dog bones in hand. He meted bones out to whomever he chose, subjectively rewarding those chosen for their attitude, talent and performance. He, as any other coach of basketball at the college level, had 200 dog bones to divide up during each game. Five is the maximum number of players on one team that can be on a basketball court at any one time during a 40 minute game. That adds up to 200 total minutes per game to be distributed between whatever combination of players a coach determines to be on the court during each minute of a game. If the coach is not feeding a player and he or she spends most of the game time on the bench, it's very challenging for that athlete. Players' reactions to the coach's not feeding them vary. Some growl, some howl, some bark, some whine and some moan. All are begging for a bone!

In the world's eye view, growing from a *dog* to a *DOG* status is solely based on the consumption of bones! Consequently the All-Americans and the All-Tournament players are well fed, getting as many as 30 or 40 bones per game. But even some of those well fed players never forgive a coach for imposed

Before being accepted into Coach Wooden's Dog Pound, proper lacing and "facing" were required. The man in charge would emerge very large through the system he lived to rule.

anorexia during the bench warming days of their development. A dog whose passion is basketball needs bones to grow mentally, physically and in proficiency.   Satiation of pride's lust to be fed through scoring and rebounding and winning is the driving force inside a developing dog. A dog's primary motivation is to get more bones.

So, what kind of a trainer was Coach Wooden to the dogs who strayed into the Bruin Pound? Most people assume that it is the dogs who are in need of training and that the coach is the best trained to function in the capacity of trainer. If that be true, then one must ask the question: Does the coach wish the dogs well? Will the coach be interested in his dogs when they are no longer pulling his sled toward championships? Is it likely that a coach can be both unselfish and successful? Doesn't a coach have to give priority to what he thinks is right to attain his goals and not concern himself about each one under his supervision as he proceeds to divvy out bones to his chosen dogs?

To win the ultimate prize in repetitive years exalts the coach above the feeders' norm.   The coach's responsibility is determining which dog to recruit and feed the optimum number of bones. Understanding why dogs were chosen and analyzing the coach's requirements for his bones reveals the coach's strategy about developing dogs. His teaching directly impacts the dogs' chances to be winners or losers in games and in life. Anyone with an interest in basketball knows the statistics that Coach John Wooden accumulated while at the helm of UCLA Basketball: 620 wins and 147 losses; 19 conference championships; 149 wins in 151 games played in Pauley Pavilion; an unprecedented ten

NCAA Championships in 12 years, including seven consecutively, with 38 straight NCAA tournament victories. However, from a DOG's perspective, a coach's win/loss record is less important than his health plan for the life of his dogs.

Coach clearly defined the benefits of bones. Their nourishment included reminders that we were students first and athletes thereafter. In the doctrine of the John R. Wooden UCLA Basketball Dog Pound Training Covenant, it ain't over until it's over. Twenty-two years after he fed me my last bone, I returned to finish my part of our agreement and graduated as a student ex-athlete from UCLA.

The question "Who is John Wooden?" assumes that I have information that others don't already have. His coaching reputation is well recorded. His Godly character is well chronicled. I am confident that when God and the Lord Jesus Christ welcome Coach into heaven, They will say, "Well done, John Robert! You did your best to train up Our DOGS that We entrusted to you at UCLA."

Who flushed the DOGS out at UCLA? It certainly was the man named John Robert Wooden who began his life on a farm near Martinsville, Indiana. I was in earnest motivated and challenged by his reward system.

The highest compliment I ever received from Coach came when I asked him to assess a pamphlet I had written. His answer was typical of Coach: "Well, Willie, you caused them to think." It took a couple of years to filter out the conclusion that I could receive his answer as a compliment. Who was the spirit behind the voice in his answer? When asked the question, "Who is John Wooden?" the most fair answer is, "Only God knows." Every experience I can remember involving Coach encouraged me to think. I could never reply conclusively to those who inquired about his religious beliefs. He never talked to me about God when I was at UCLA. Neither did he publicly credit God or Jesus Christ with being the source of what he taught or lived. He caused me to wonder, *Who was the source of his dad's organized thoughts that he carried around on a little piece of paper in his wallet since his youth? Were all of his teachings from a traceable source?* I have concluded that Coach always "did his best" to encourage everyone in his sphere of influence "to do his or her best." That Spirit behind his teaching voice is a Godly One in him.

Canine Rivalry: Dining, Whining and Howling

A member of the Fab Five of UCLA's first NCAA Championship team wrote to me that he thought some readers of a letter I had written to selected basketball alumni might conclude that I thought Coach a racist. As part of his pious lecture, he challenged my Christian ethics. In a tone which breathed heavily of wallowing in its own hypocrisy, his thumb reflected back into his eye the Biblical plank of his finger pointing judgment. I received his comments in the spirit of his concerned but misplaced notion of protecting Coach.

The content of my letter to "Selected UCLA Basketball Alumni" had boiled over and out of me after many years of simmering in silence. I was relieved by speaking out in constructive criticism. Adopted children of a successful common father are always vying for his love and attention. Some even stoop to tattle-tale tactics to plead for a bone. Since his adoptions occurred over a 27 year period, most of Coach's boys don't know anything about the personalities of the others; yet we identify with the homeland of Bruin Hoop under our coaching father, John Robert Wooden. We individually reserve the right to say anything we deem appropriate to any of our Bruin siblings to their faces and in full view of other family members. So I said what I had to say in my initial letter about one I surmised was full of himself at the expense of all of us. This other dog's response to my letter was received in its intent and his convictions will fall back dead in the Wooden Dog Pound's pile of unsuccessful appeals to be *Coach's favorite.*

In the mid-1970s I approached Coach Wooden to grant my business associates and me the exclusive right to market him and his image to the masses. I had a group of millionaire alumni professionals who were eager to share Coach's message with people around the world. I was concerned about protecting Coach from his naïveté and complete lack of interest in money matters. I felt that he needed to shield his legacy's value from eager and greedy speculators. He had advised me during negotiations with pro basketball owners at the end of my college career to "take whatever they offer you and be grateful."

One of the **lessons** I learned early in life was to "make your deal going in" because you have to live with that deal when you want to get out. My mom taught me that a godly man must honor his word above all his name. It's not an emotional issue; it's a legal issue. I posited that Coach's unselfishness would be of greater benefit to his posterity if his name and fame were framed legally to ensure control by his family. Simply put, we were prepared to make sure that Coach Wooden's posterity would be the caretakers of his name and legacy forever. We proposed to form two entities: John Robert Wooden, Inc., a business venture to trademark his name and market the Pyramid of Success, his various writings and his father's seven-point creed, and Coach John R. Wooden Foundation, a non-profit vehicle for philanthropy and sharing his philosophy with future generations.

Coach thanked me and said that he had been asked previously by another of his players to do some promotional projects but had turned him down. "It wouldn't be fair to my other boys" was his logic. During the next 30 years I watched with much interest the decisions Coach made about associating his name and image with promoters and venture capitalists.

A recent article in the *Los Angeles Times* (27 August 2005) has made it abundantly clear that my concerns were well founded. For the past thirty years, Coach has participated in the presentation of the John R. Wooden Award, honoring annually collegiate basketball's top players. Members of the Los Angeles Athletic Club became concerned that its ownership of the John R. Wooden Award arising from its trademark of Coach's name was diminished because Coach had decided to align his name with another athletic award. Now, after years of allowing others to have control of the use of his honored name, Coach has apparently come to the conclusion I shared with him in the 1970s – that he and his family should make legal decisions about and bene-fit from the legacy he has built through his life's work and reputation – as he said, "I don't think it's right the athletic club wants complete use of my name." Had his name been protected as I suggested,

Team Reunion at the Naming of the Nell & John Wooden Court, December 2004

Ben Rogers • Willie Naulls • Bob Archer • Bill Eblen • Nolan Johnson • Morris Taft • Carroll Adams • Dick "Skeets" Banton

Photo courtesy of Michael Warren

Coach and his family would have benefited from the *gross* of many endeavors, not the *net crumbs*.

From a distance, Coach Wooden's various expressions appear to be repetitious but all have exploited his winning record and his message of developing faith in oneself through living the teaching of his Pyramid of Success. Coach specifically shared his Pyramid and philosophy, but not his religious beliefs, with his teams and audiences. Most recently he has attempted to share his religious faith, which had been withheld previously in the spirit of privacy. So the glory shifted from him and his success model teaching to God as his source. In retrospect, I don't know, as one of his players, how I would have reacted to him if he had included the teachings of Jesus among his repetitious one-liners.

Mom's **Lessons** taught me, "If a man thinks, speaks and does only good, he got it from God. Only God is good and God is the only One who can give a man of His good to share with others." Coach's responses to my questions encouraged me to think about what I am confronted with in my relationships with all people and make up my mind how to interpret and react to their actions.

The mounting puppy stories over the years reveal the ongoing drama scripted by the individual drive within each Bruin dog to get close to the Trainer. Only an insider would be sensitive to the unfolding dramas. Toward the end of 2004, Pauley Pavilion's basketball court was appropriately named the Nell and John Wooden Court. There were as many Wooden dogs in attendance as could make it and we were all salivating in Coach's glory – just sniffing for the semblance of a bone. It's not playing time any more. It's proximity to participate in his fame time. As was the case with Abraham and Job of Biblical lore, Coach is being more abundantly blessed of God in his later years than he was during his "prime time years." From all over the world he receives invitations to do book deals and requests to teach how he inspired his dogs to perform for his glory. Thank God he is finally paid handsomely. Every time he chooses someone outside his family Pound to share our bones, there is howling, barking, whining and even resentment.

At the UCLA vs. Michigan State basketball game on Saturday, December 20, 2004, the day of the court naming ceremony, a Bruin Basketball Commemorative Program publication was circulated and contained a well written article by a fellow dog: "Mr. Wooden Goes to Washington." After the author's description of how he and his wife were honored to be included at Coach's invitation as he received the Presidential Medal of Freedom, he said something very thought provoking in his closing remarks, and I quote: "How was I lucky enough to be invited along for this magical event I'll never know. But as Coach has taught me, giving to others with no thought of receiving anything in return is the greatest gift of all."

I thought that to be a contrived summation of a Biblical principle for which few give God the credit as author. Was he speaking of *his* "giving to others"? I wonder what Andre McCarter thought as he read his canine brother's remarks. After all, it was Andre who instigated and, over many years, labored for Coach to receive this highest civilian award. I can only surmise that Coach and his family had no clue that Andre, more than anyone else, had solicited the participation of all of us Bruin Dogs who wrote in support of Andre's proposed candidacy of Coach

John Robert Wooden. It's less challenging to wax eloquent about the teaching philosophy of men as one enjoys the fruit of their fame than it is to sit at home and observe the public accolades about something one has wholeheartedly promoted and, by faith, claimed through patient perseverance without sharing in its glorious meal. I would have loved to have read in that Bruin publication that Mr. and Mrs. Andre McCarter had shared in the ceremony in which the President of our country honored Coach. Not as a Black skin/White skin thing as some of my Dog-Pounders might conclude, but as God commands us: "Render therefore to all their due: taxes to whom taxes are due, customs to whom customs, fear to whom fear, **honor to whom honor**" (Romans 13:7, NKJV).

I am also compelled to include my thoughts on the frenzy to be near Coach at the dedication of the UCLA basketball court. We were at it again, vying for position to be fed some of his bones. Bones of fame are now about money, recognition and reputation, not playing time. I know because I have been bombarded by authors, publishers and deal makers who appeal to me to share – in writing, and at my expense – my experiences with Coach for their own book deals. They want me to share our environmental secrets about what it meant to be a Dog Pound member at UCLA under Coach. They assume that they can exploit the notion that I have been taught well by Coach's example "to give to others with no thought of receiving anything in return." Coach has always responded positively to my requests of him, which have almost always involved my ministry work with youth. I must always remind myself that God is in control and

His will is to bless Coach's overall agenda at large. So the court was dedicated and the dogs were relegated to being Coach John Robert Wooden's DOGS. Yes, we were – and still are – DOGS.

Who flushed the dogs out? We are an organism, not an organization, and we live to exercise our freedom of thought and expression, individually. What breed would you ascribe to your favorite Bruin dog? Doberman Pinscher . . . Chihuahua . . . Greyhound . . . Rottweiler . . . Akita . . . Pit Bull . . . the barkless Basenji?

The wisdom in Coach's strategy of inspiring me to think is that it incited me to meditate and look for the source of his philosophy. God has said through Solomon, "There is nothing new under the sun." He also said through Jesus that "[God's] Word is Truth." Coach directly embodied dignity's purpose by inspiring all dogs to not think of themselves as basketball players only. He never did for me what I could figure out for myself.

An examination of dogs' fruit can give insight into a coach's true character. The players are a testimony to the coach's input. At each UCLA player's departure, the question becomes for each dog to answer, What am I prepared to do with the advantage that I received from bones fed me by Coach Wooden? I lusted for, fought for and got my share of *dem bones*. Early on in my career at UCLA, I barked, howled, sulked and even ran away from UCLA's Pound because I thought Coach had unfairly given someone else my bones. But, praise God for His mercy! Coach hooked me back up to his sled for the remainder of my eligibility. The training and nourishment from his bones flushed out of us Foundational Bruin Dogs individual confidence to work out of ourselves what God had planted in us at birth. The rich and diverse heritage of the UCLA DOG POUND is permanently set on a course of excellence.

Lesson: Mom taught me, "To whom much is given, much is required."

My Personal Howl

Hate melts down one's spirit and soul. The implosion resulting from hatred causes debilitating landslides within. A silent killer thrives on words and actions of the hating heart, oftentimes unknowingly, working against itself. In many instances I stumbled into the pit which hate had dug for me. The most challenging move of faith for me was to trust the soul of Coach Wooden, not knowing who he was apart from his looks. The Black skin/White skin thing was resting heavily on my mind and I couldn't kick the feeling. After attempting several times to tell Coach how I felt inside about that "staying in my place" thing, I got the vibe to just shut up and grow up! I kept hinting, but I sensed I was talking to myself in rhetorical echo. Not telling him the simple truth in some notion of patronizing respect crippled our relationship. Because of shallow communication, we were destined to be on spiritual crutches, a condition which, from my perspective, hasn't been corrected even now.

Over the years I concluded that I was the one who should have initiated conversation. Maybe I thought I never earned his respect. I know that he has always respected my right to choose who I wanted to develop into through my decisions. And maybe that's enough. This realization soothed the rage which occasionally heated my inner logic about Coach. I have always sensed a spiritual grafting in attachment at the hip to Coach and I have heard a similar perspective from others of his players. My challenge has been that I wanted to hear his desire to remain connected. Writing on the issue has unmasked my speculation on his thoughts.

My life has been one in the trenches of competition's earned growth. Cheating was counter productive to my growth and I paid the price when I succumbed to its seduction. Reasoning with myself, I surmised that I couldn't grow if I allowed hatred to hang around. When I harbored hate, my mother's **Lessons** reminded me that I was on the road to the devil's home in hell. Hate and rage put me in a self-constructed cage. When I didn't get an award for what I believed to be superior achievement, my insides churned like a mixer, but my expression was rehearsed through the teachings of John Wooden and my mom: "No one should be able to tell what you are feeling." The strong, silent Willie had grown up and was back to being seen and not heard.

I survived the self-imposed pain of my UCLA decisions. When I was not chosen to go to the Olympics and when my jersey was not retired, I experienced deeply rooted pain like nothing I had felt before. Perhaps it was a matter of thinking of myself more highly than I ought to have. That was pain. It hurt me deeper than I could bear and I had no one to talk to but myself. Ding-dong – Mom's bells went off again. "You're never alone. God is right there with you." Later in my life, I thought that a Godly man moves on and doesn't concern himself with such trivia. True! Through serving others, especially youth and their families, I forgot to think about myself. I could only write this book when I stopped to think about what I could say in response to God's mandate that would benefit others trapped in the mire of self pity.

I speak from the inner sanctuary of the God kind of faith that nothing in me hates. Hate used up more of my life than I could spare. Rage in me has never been out of its cage, but he sometimes barks loudly to remind me of his presence. Again this Black skin/White skin thing rests heavily on my mind. Now, it is the evil that I hate – as God hates evil. Through my eyes alone, I have seen the reaction of White skin to me and others of my skin color. I have learned to discern the gaze from behind the lenses of a confronted other, whether friend or brother or foe. Some are White and some are Black – from head to toe. To encircle them all with God's Love is the daily challenge of this UCLA Hall of Fame Dog.

Induction into the
UCLA Athletics Hall of Fame

1986

Jonah • Anne • Willie • Malaika

The joy and elation in the eyes of my wife, son and daughter tell the story of family identification with public recognition of my earned accomplishments.

Recruiting: Beginning on a Sandy Foundation
My Way or Mom's Way?

Over the years I have heard Coach Wooden's public comments about some of his boys' exaggerating the number of schools recruiting them out of high school. I am confident that he didn't know that Stanford University offered a private school option for my consideration which would have accommodated my less than readily admissible academic status into UCLA. The University of California at Berkeley (Cal) was up front and serious with anyone who would listen that I was their man. I was told that local colleges and universities were discouraged by a sportswriter's projection that all of the first team All-City basketball players in 1952 had committed to attending UCLA. However, scholarship offers came to me from northern and southern California, Oregon, Washington and from other states that wanted to test their segregated waters with Willie Naulls' big toe.

The meaning of the word "scholarship" was incompletely introduced to me by a college coach who offered me one after seeing me play in a basketball tournament when I was in the ninth grade. The true meaning of the word began to unfold in real life negotiations during my senior year in high school. This was all new to me. My responsibility in decision making raised its head. People were bidding for my talent but didn't think I knew it. Every school's representative reminded me that I

Coach John Wooden
The Recruiter

1952

I often had to remind myself of this
Recruiting Smile

was Black skinned and that few people of my color had the opportunity they were presenting to me. Soon I had to make a decision based on my evaluation of people, information about their schools, their academic and athletic programs, my gut sense about the honesty of the basketball coach and, in the final analysis, where I really wanted to go to school. Over the years my mom had convinced me that I couldn't make a wrong decision if I were led by God. "All things work to the good of those who love the Lord and are called according to His purpose" (Romans 8:28). I was well prepared to make a decision and stick by what I chose to do.

In negotiating my scholarship, I learned the word "reimbursement." Agents from interested schools used that word, with emphasis. Soon the word "allowances" was added, with meaning, to my vocabulary. Put into the context of talent bartering, each school's representative made it very clear that I would be reimbursed for air travel, meals, local and away ground transportation and for all incidentals – allowances related to being recruited. After a few days of throwing these words around, Mom really nailed me to my cross with her question: "Your changing attitude doesn't have anything to do with a love of money, William, does it?"

I thought to myself, *She doesn't understand.* I was convinced that none of these people would have spoken to me if I didn't play basketball better than anyone around. I'm sure she knew that I thought Willie's Wisdom in this negotiating arena was more informed than hers. I was on a different road now. I had experienced great joy and a sense of independence in earnestly working for money of my own. Her query caused me to question everyone's motives. I was given reimbursement money but also money with some undeclared strings firmly attached. Mom probably knew what I was thinking: Why is this man giving me money? How much more will he give up? How much am I worth to them? This was easy money.

My mother asked me what I would do when someone offered me more money than the last person. She told me to go to college where I was comfortable and to never forget that they stopped auctioning off slaves years ago. "Aren't you allowing yourself to be put back on that auction block again, William? Don't be bought by the highest bidder, William, because schools can't offer you any more than is allowed, can they? I know that you will not be lured into doing wrong by making a decision based on getting something that's illegal. Go to the school that you want to but make sure you go there because that is where you really want to go. Don't choose a school because someone offers you something more than is right. Does every school offer the same amount of extra meal money when you go on these trips to their campuses?"

"No, Mama!"

"How much extra money did UCLA give you for meals when you visited them?"

"None, Mama! But, Mom, this is California, and don't you think I should know how much they will pay?"

She squared off in front of me, gazing into my eyes which were shifting away from the smile coming forth. "You know the answer to that question. Where would you go to school if you could get money off your brain?"

I said, "Mom, they brought the subject up so I

just want to find out what I'm worth to them before I commit. They won't tell me anything unless I ask each the same questions. These schools are never in the same room at the same time."

Mom dropped her head and said, "Where in the world did you get the idea that you could get more for playing basketball by playing one school against the other?"

"That's not what I'm doing, Ma. You don't understand. I am on the meat market, so shouldn't I try to get the most I can – per pound – for this Black meat?"

She walked away a few steps, turned and spoke. "I raised you different from that, son. Go to school where you want to go to school, even if we have to pay for it." She then came back toward me, her gaze fixed. "That's not the issue here." She pulled my head down by my shirt to whisper in my ear. "What are you worth to yourself? Rid your mind of how much money you can get and place the value on where you want to go to be educated."

"OK, Mom!" I stared at her in silence, finally adding that I had been told that it cost UCLA only $32.50 per semester for my scholarship's tuition. "What's wrong with me taking a little money for out of pocket expenses?" We were squaring off to frame my independence declaration.

She looked deep into my eyes and said, "Hear these last words of advice from me. Your tone tells me that you have made up your mind to get all you can get from playing basketball in college. If you think you know it all, you are off on the wrong road already. What you can learn from this point on from people who have your best interest at heart will begin when you stop and acknowledge that the amount of money you can get is not of any importance. The question is, has the money got you? I'll tell you for the last time: Choose a school that you would go to if you didn't play basketball. Choose a school where you see in people that they genuinely wish you well. I'll tell you how to free yourself to make an uninfluenced decision. Give every penny back to those folk who gave you extra money. Then you will be free to make a decision that's right for you."

Her words shook me to my roots. She raised me to be free to choose who could influence me. "OK, Mama."

She drove with me to a building on Wilshire Boulevard, in or near Beverly Hills. We parked in its parking lot and entered through the front lobby. The security guard/host near the elevator stopped us, asking, "May I help you?"

"My mom and I are here to visit someone on the executive floor," was my reply. When I gave the president's name, the man's facial expression changed from *What in the world does this 6'6" Black kid and this 5'5 1/2" Black woman want – to – Oh, you must be that great high school athlete. Let me take you upstairs to his office.*

The elevator door opened up into a lobby with offices in either direction. We turned right through double glass doors and toward the smiles of three men and their executive secretary. After I introduced them to Mom, they led us into a large, lavishly furnished office. They talked nervously for a few minutes about how happy they were to have me drop by unexpectedly to say hello. Then the question was posed, "How can we help you today, Willie? Are you ready to sign to attend our great university?"

I stood up, pulled out a wad of cash which was the exact amount that he had slipped into my hand the last time we had seen each other and handed it to him. "My mother doesn't think that I should accept this money, and neither do I."

His face drained of blood. He choked a bit and then spoke. "Well, the money was so you wouldn't have to spend your own in case you decided to visit me or the school again." That seemed logical to me, but . . . .

I thanked him and we departed the way we had entered. Mom never said a word but she had this smile on her face which I knew meant I had done all right. She finally said, "You bought your freedom back. Now you are free to decide where you want to go to school." I didn't know exactly what she meant, but I did know that I felt a lot lighter without all that cash in my pocket. What price freedom?

I also detected for the first time a slight resentment toward my mom. She had encouraged me to give back about fifteen hundred dollars in lean green. The twinge in my soul was a pivot away from the straight and narrow of her **Lessons**. I thought about that money for a few weeks after giving it up. A voice whispered, "How long would you have to work to save up $1,500? Don't you deserve it after all the hard work and accomplishments?"

Mom's Voice interrupted, "Auctions for slaves were outlawed years ago. Do you want to sell yourself, William, to the highest bidder?"

This was my final gesture to include Mom in my decisions. I knew already what she would choose. It was always God's Way. "What about the FUN way, Mom?" I asked.

She said, "There is no greater joy than doing it God's Way."

"OK, Mom, I've got to go!" Giving that money back was a relief for her but a challenge for me. In my heart I wanted to keep every dime they greased my palm with.

I took Mom's advice and chose the university of my first choice, UCLA, then expected them to match every promise I had received from any other university. All of them taught me the words "out of pocket allowances for reimbursable expenses." I sensed a compromising shift in my thinking. Why did the NCAA decide to limit how much student athletes could earn? Why limit what we got for allowances? Ostensibly they were controlling to protect smaller schools and their bottom line, but who decided that all student athletes had to live below the poverty level? My attitude didn't sit well with Coach Wooden and my reputation gradually turned into that of a hustler. I expected to get the best, highest paying jobs during vacations and summertime, rationalizing that I was a better, more responsible worker than anyone before me. I learned from bragging White players I met during recruiting days that there were jobs – and then there were J-O-B-S which paid much more money than the jobs. They all filled my brain with superlatives so I was convinced that I was high priced Black meat.

Arriving on campus my first semester, I was still driven by the desire to get even financially. I devised a scheme to enroll in eighteen to twenty units of classes, buy the required books, and take the receipts to the Athletic Department to be reimbursed. Then I systematically dropped most of the classes, sold the books back to the bookstore and kept the refunds. Mom was right. Money had me. I was convinced that the University and its Athletic Department had deceived me and owed me something since I, ostensibly, had passed up opportunities to be more liberally reimbursed for out of pocket reasonable and allowable expenses. Oh, what a wretched jock I was – or was on the road to becoming.

Professional men who said they were UCLA representatives lied to me and did not honor every verbal commitment of a full four-year scholarship. They lied to me! Every time I saw those same representatives with other recruits I went the opposite direction. My mother taught me, "If you don't have anything good to say about someone, shut up." I attempted to broach the subject with Coach and discovered he had taken the righteous position of not knowing what everyone had said to me, but he offered "the NCAA Rules."

I am not using their deceitfulness as an excuse for my attitude. Some of the decisions I made as an undergraduate student athlete at UCLA were bad ones. Some may perceive my suggestion of recruiters' deceit as whining in many of the things I say. My words should not be interpreted as an attempt to justify my choices. There were circumstances out of my control that influenced my decisions. My *"You owe me, UCLA"* conviction was a bad choice which tainted my attitude and negatively influenced my academic pursuit of real scholarship excellence. After all is said about this matter of athletic endeavor, the real purpose of attending universities is the pursuit of maturity through academic and social enterprise. Mama was right again but I didn't hear her voice often. The roar of the crowd and my growing and hostile ego squeezed to near closure the pathway of reason to my soul. I responded to what I perceived to be injustice. Reacting rebelliously, I became the product of my choices: a lying, deceitful, selfishly motivated, underproductive athlete who used UCLA's systems as I perceived they used me.

UCLA rated my student athletic achievement as competitively great, but in my heart I knew where Mom stood on the issue. From time to time I offered her some of my earnings. She advised me to put whatever I had left in the bank in the event of rainy days.

Lesson: To all of you future college athletic scholarship recipients: Only deal with your future coach in the presence of the school's athletic director. Open and earnest communication between the athlete (talent) and the coach (authority) before the athletic director (university representative) can eliminate misunderstandings and dramatically impact the athlete's holistic development.

The Law of Self Preservation

When I was under my mother's rule
Self Preservation she taught me for school
"Everything in life," she said, "is at stake"
Even the quality of it – my decision to make
I was to decide where and how I would live
and who would be my neighbor's keeper –
    to give
Total commitment I must put on the line
in the environment where I choose to
    incline
I must invest my heart's passion
in whatever I choose to fashion
The Law of Self Preservation I thought a
    must
to guard every degree of giving my trust!
God's first law of nature
on the lips of every sage
instructs me to choose His Wisdom for my
    journey
or fall victim to the lure in evil's cage

My Last Encounter with Dad

The summer between high school and college passed in the fullness of work and play. A UCLA alumnus in the construction business hired me as a laborer. My first assignment was to dig the basement of a new bank to be erected on Long Beach Boulevard in Downey, California. Manual became this laborer's game and I thought it less challenging carrying hod up and down ladders to the masons than working in Dallas as an ice man's helper. As the weeks progressed I was the manual for all labors to be done. I did my best – with enthusiasm. Two consecutive days of handling a jack hammer during my third week on the job was a bigger challenge than the fifty pound block of ice had been on my seven year old body back there in Dallas. *Hammer time* pushed me and shook me to my jarred limits. By the middle of the third day, I finally had to ask the superintendent for mercy. A couple more days would pass before my equilibrium allowed me to do any athletic activity.

Armed with the money I earned that summer and my "stash," Mom and I did college time shopping together during late August. She was also present at my first automobile acquisition. It was a used two-door navy blue 1950 Ford. Having my own wheels for the first time was almost as liberating as leaving Dallas and arriving in San Pedro. I picked up a girl and went out on a date for the first time in my own car at the age of 17. It's impossible for any of you to know what that experience meant to me. Or, maybe you too have

Graduation from San Pedro High School
June 1952

experienced the joy of eating the fruit of hard work's cumulative rewards.

My father called me into his presence after I had put the last items of clothing into my car before departing for UCLA. He said, "I don't want you to forget; that car that you bought is our car. Everything you have and will have is ours, not yours alone." At that moment I realized that I hadn't looked into his eyes during my high school years. The thought of ignoring him passed when I realized that he was dead serious. Before I could turn and walk out to avoid the confrontation, he raised his voice to clarify his stance. "Do you understand me, boy?"

I knew this was it. With a slight air of self confidence and in the clarity of finality, I said, "The truth is, Dad, this car is not our car but my car. Everything inside the car is mine and you don't own any part of it. I don't owe you anything and I don't want anything from you." My mom and siblings were right there, present to say goodbye. They didn't expect this grandstand play that my father was attempting.

Like a released spring, he leapt to his feet, ripping his belt from around his waist. He lashed out at me in all of his pent up fury. The belt hit my left arm and wrapped around twice as I pulled it out of his hand into mine. We had a long overdue stare-down. I didn't give an inch of jack hammer earned space and my self indignation moved forward across the line of verbal confrontation. He uttered a retreating "I guess it's time for you to get on out of my house."

My dear Mom tried to cut short this final solution but could only watch as I threw the belt on the couch and headed for the door. My eyes never left his and I saw him blink and shift his gaze sideways and then downward as if to assess what his bluff had accomplished. "I guess it is time and I'm out of here" was my departing retort, unbecoming of what Mom had taught me.

Take – Care for Yourself

Take – Care for Yourself
WORDS empathic and sincere
voiced from the heart of my mother
deposited into my soul's bank
as I ventured beyond her cover

Take – Care for Yourself
Let no one intrude
in – to contaminate your body and soul
It's evil who contends for your spirit
with self implosion its ultimate goal

Take – Care for Yourself
There was confidence in her gentle push
which fused my psyche's primal rush
by preparing me for the long haul from the
    beginning
and planting me in the mortar of
    accountability
Mom empowered me with God's formula
    for winning

Take – Care for Yourself
A blessed Seed slanting
which settled into God's Tree planting
producing Seed bearing fruit – granting
a sharing with others of faith's ranting

Mom and my younger brother came out to the car to "wish me well" at UCLA. As I was driving away I thought for the first time that there were two members of my family who did wish me well – Mom and Jerry, who was three years younger than I. He had always been eager to know if our high school teams had won and how many points I had scored during basketball season or how many hits I had and strike-outs I pitched during baseball season. During his high school years at Fremont, Jerry didn't play varsity basketball because he matured late. While in the United States Armed Services, he grew to 6' 2" and became quite a competitive basketball player around Los Angeles in his twenties and thirties. He and his summer league team absolutely wiped out a team which included Woody Sauldsberry (a pro with the Philadelphia 76ers) and me. Jerry and his friend Taylor boasted for years that, if Woody and I were pros and their team beat us so soundly, "Well, we must be All-World." I loved my brother Jerry. Although we very seldom talked about our personal lives, I knew for sure that he wished me well.

I have long given up on trying to understand Dad's obvious frustration about my leaving his house. Who was to be the authority in my life when I left home that day of last confrontation? Was I finally in control of my own destiny? Since junior high school I had paid my own way in almost every area of my life except housing. I'll never forget that my friend George Padovan's mom fed me baked albacore tuna when I was starving in high school, as did Pepi from the kitchen of his Pepi Pal's Café in San Pedro. Pepi's beef stew was addictive and I know his profits went down during my senior year.

Many other people in San Pedro contributed to my benefit and I am eternally grateful. The challenge of self confidence was very real as I moved from the security of the San Pedro community and my primary family group to the UCLA Basketball family group. I thought to myself that the only group leader at UCLA who wanted me as a family member was Coach Wooden.

Leaving my parents' nest was more of a mental challenge than it should have been. I soon learned that housing was the biggest challenge for an African American student who wanted to live on or near the UCLA campus. The University was in the middle of an exclusively White business and residential territory and I was an invader. I approached Westwood cautiously as though I were moving back to the South. Those folk who had recruited me had promised verbally, regarding the terms of my scholarship, that I would be taken care of as no other before me had been. *"No problema, Willie, no problema!"*

It was an unsettling experience. I was raised to not expect the whole truth and nothing but the truth from anybody, but especially White Men. I was prepared for the whole truth. The pressing question that I had was, What is the truth about where I will live? "Willie, we will match any offer you have from another school. Coach Wooden thinks you are the finest prospect he has seen and we all want you to be a Bruin. You will get the finest education available anywhere and your ROOM, BOARD, TUITION, BOOKS AND EXPENSES will be paid for by UCLA – in full. *NO PROBLEMA!"* Coach Wooden, I assumed thereafter, never knew or agreed to these broad strokes of the negotiating brush – only UCLA's agents. He must have known about the housing situation in Westwood. Three out of five was the best they did to fulfill their promises to me. I did not have the luxury of a "normal campus living environment" provided for me.

I am reminded of one of my mother's favorite proclamations: "Prayer changes things." When I decided to accept a UCLA athletic scholarship, it never occurred to me that I would not be allowed to live in Westwood or on campus. When I visited UC Berkeley, the student athletes took me to the apartment on campus where I would live. As a student athlete at UCLA, the Watts to Westwood trek was a daily 30- to 40-mile round-trip, unless, of course, there was truth to the changing of "things" as declared over my life by my mother. Bettie Arlene Artis Naulls always saw those things that were not as though they were, as prayers answered when she prayed, until their full manifestation, through patient perseverance in what God's Word says.

What happened astonished even those in charge of and responsible to the law of the Westwood covenants. Even when there was no worldly provision made for me or my look-alikes, God provided. My charge from Mom was "make yourself useful" and I had, through many hours of devoted practice and on-the-job experience in athletics. Coach Wooden appealed to residents in the geographical area of UCLA (and I paraphrase), "Somebody, make room for Willie! If we are going to win, we need him if we are to compete with USC, Washington, Cal, the University of San Francisco (USF) and other national powers." The Good

Samaritan was initially Ed Hummell, UCLA's Head Cheerleader, who invited me into his home on San Vicente between Olympic and Wilshire Boulevards near the Beverly Hills city border. That wasn't bad for a start!!

Ed's parents honored their son's imposition and were very cordial, but I'm sure they questioned the sanity of his choice. He challenged them to demonstrate their professed love for him. Ed, I believe, was living in his chosen fraternity on campus. Imagine for a second this possible scenario: He picks up the telephone and says, *Mom, there's this big kid who Coach Wooden says needs a place to stay and Negroes can't rent a room in Westwood. Mom, can you convince Dad to make room for Willie? I don't quite know how to pronounce his last name, but I'm told he is a Christian, soft spoken young man, AND . . . the boy can really play basketball, Mom! And Mom, he's from Watts in South Central L.A. And, Mom, he is a Negro kid. But Mom, he can really play basketball!!* Would you like to have been there to hear Ed's father's response when he was approached by his dear wife? I imagine he said something like, *What has Ed done to us now? I thought he was out of here and now, as a joke, he's sending us a kid from Watts! God Almighty, help us!* Well, they took me in, and all these many years have passed and I'm still thankful to them and to Ed for acting on Coach's request that they make room for me.

It took me about thirty minutes to drive from our home in Watts to Mr. and Mrs. Hummell's home. I would stay there until Coach found me a permanent residence near the UCLA campus. He knew all summer that I was coming. Was he prepared for the stubbornness of racial separation?

Patience was a part of Mom's teaching, so I was prepared for any situation. I reviewed in my mind the **Lessons** she taught me. Four lines from Mom's **Lessons** were branded loud and clear in the focus of my thoughts as I turned into the Hummels' driveway. I was ready for any challenge.

Care for yourself and your personal hygiene.
Live by the Standard of our Lord Supreme.
Study in school; observe the Word of Faith's
   test.
Compete with yourself alone to be God's
   best.

Soon thereafter, led by their president, Sam Silber, a fraternity of young Jewish students, located on property near that of Ed's fraternity on the UCLA campus, relieved Ed's family and took on the burden and responsibility of neighborly love. Diversity began therein through daily exposure and 24 hour days of living, sleeping, dining, and sharing of family values and histories. The Judeo-Christian love was God at work there in the ΣAM house although none of us even suspected that truth.

Prayer does change things, for all of us. In their simple empathic act of giving me a place to live in the middle of Westwood, my soul became more settled, awakened and committed to the idea of having a family and raising them up in that UCLA community. Years later, after my professional basketball career and graduation, I bought a home on Loring Avenue, two blocks east of UCLA and four blocks south of Sunset Boulevard. All of my children went to local schools, public and private, in the Westwood area. The UCLA campus was our backyard, playground, resource, cultural and entertainment center, as it had been in earlier years for my wife. Anne graduated from UCLA's undergraduate and medical school programs and her parents both worked for the University – her father, John Randolph Van de Water, as a law professor and her mother, Harriet Doll Van de Water, as a financial aid counselor for the various professional school students.

I am a witness. My Mother's Prayers to God over my life came to full fruition. As my life's direction was set on course by the Lessons she taught me, the Holy Spirit's Power influenced specific individuals in the UCLA environment whom God chose to assist me along my trek. I was set free to work out of myself what God had put into me – to glorify Him. God is always at His work, working *in the process* of maturing His Word in believers' lives.

PRAYER CHANGES THINGS!

In the Process

In the Process
Ongoing themes
stitching the seams
of the garment of life for to wear
Striving and working
molding the character
illuminates the cross for to bear

Midday slumber
lack of focus is the number
How important is the work – to do?
Tallying what's abounding
encouraging the floundering
like scores of others in life's zoo

Misguided muscles
en route to their tussles
thoughts of pleasure being their guide
Fad laden dreams
chasing temporary schemes
stopping to let a breath hitch a ride

Tomorrow's thinking
what to see through the blinking
on the road of challenge's pursuit
Evolving maze of procession
dawning a symphonic repression
Don't want to be another loser's recruit

In the Process
is worked out through moving
what ever else you want to be ensuing
off the stalemate of your indecision's
        coup-ing
Don't let idleness's progress remain
stuck in the mire of your indecision's
        domain
Walk in God's faith of In the Process's
        Proclaim

UCLA and the Jews Who Took Me Inn

I enjoyed and greatly benefited from my experience of living in a Jewish fraternity house for over half of my college days. The association challenged me in the game of life to grow through the invisible walls which were erected as mental barriers to deny me my equal rights. As far as I could determine, most of UCLA tolerated Jews because they had White skin and were competitively qualified for admission into the academic system of this statewide public institution. Some called them niggers with white skin – who let me live inn – because of the talent God placed within – me. The situation began in sin, as I was denied housing because of the color of my skin, but God turned my experiences into a growth of WIN-WIN! I've been around people who talked about Jews in the same derogatory manner as they talked about me to them. Where do you think the term "forked tongue" evolved out of? That's not a White thing alone, but an evil counterfeit of contrived utterance. Evil's intent desires the color of anyone's skin to wear, to pollute the lenses of seeing for the hearers to bear.

The Lesson that I learned living in the Sigma Alpha Mu (ΣAM) house with the "Sammies" was the direct correlation between academic preparation and academic achievement. Going to class was not very high on my agenda, so I was not prepared for most of my exams. My grade point average was barely high enough to keep me eligible for sports. Honoring my part in our scholarship covenant, to sit at the feet and learn from great teachers to earn an

Richard Agay	Herman Ballin	Ivan Berger	Robert Behar
Jack Blum	David Bromberg	Bob Browne	Burton Chudacoff
Ronald Feldman	Sanford Fine	Barry Finkelstein	Jerry Fox
Dan Goldberg	Stuart Groboyes	Ben Greene	Stuart Hackel

Sigma Alpha Mu

1953

The Jews who took me Inn

academic degree from UCLA, was never a part of my thinking process. Playing basketball was the only hard work that I diligently and joyfully pursued during my time there. I was honored with Coach Wooden's **Competitive Greatness** type awards for my All-American efforts in basketball.

The university honored its commitment to open its classroom doors and pay for any courses and degree pursuits of my choosing. I took the easy road, fulfilling the dumb jock image. Jocks are demanded to put their quality time in the short run of their sport's life. Youth who want role models to emulate should pay more attention to those men and women whose long range goals of mental and spiritual development are committed to a professional field of their passion. Working at becoming your best in sports is a short run pursuit toward a goal of competitive greatness which requires that you give the prime of yourself to achieve that greatness. That's what doing your best means: Giving Your All. Few men and women achieve excellence of academic scholarship during an All-American athletic career. Those who do are truly motivated to prepare themselves at all times to be at their best at any time and deserve special recognition.

Back at the Sammie house, I learned terms like *anti-Semite* and *bias* and *the Arabs* and how to pray in Hebrew before meals as a normal part of daily living. My world had expanded from Dallas, where Black skin was hated by White skin – to a negotiated position of "Let's Make a Deal." Willie Naulls was asked by UCLA, "So, what can you do for us?" My reputation in competitive athletics responded, "I can do basketball very well – and to your gain." The Sammies said, "OK, we'll help you

Don Block   Charles Sanders   Samuel Silber   Roy Kates
Robert Reinstein   Barry Silverman   Marshall Siskin   Robert Leib
Al Gilens   Louis Sobel   Roger Steinberg   Mark Rich
Robert Kay   Steve Totterman   Jack Turk

Sam Silber, the Sammies' President
(top row, third from left)

and I met for the first time in Coach Wooden's
office. He brought the Good News from his
ΣAM brothers that they had voted to take me in.
I was no longer a scholarshipped street person.

both by housing this experiment." We had a deal.

My soul was a sponge that needed time to evaluate and appreciate the acculturation. The genetic mix of my body was unchanged, but my spirit awakened in me a desire to work to afford material things. The young men around me had families and communities who served them. Most of the students I met at UCLA were provided an affluent socio-economic environment where they could learn and become accredited professionals who would someday provide for and lead their families and communities. Most, if not all, of the Sammies became successful professionals whose quality of life was determined, or at least strongly influenced, by what they learned as we shared living space at UCLA. I first heard and used the word "networking" there.

None of the Jewish young men with whom I lived in the ΣAM house participated on a UCLA athletic team, although Norm Jacobs became UCLA's head cheerleader. I experienced what they went through, studying to get themselves qualified for professional schools. Over twenty years later, at a convenient time, I imitated their acts of persistent perseverance and became a graduate of UCLA. I enjoyed that pursuit as much as and maybe even more than the pursuit of glory and fame in sports. The competition was the same, against myself alone, to do my best academically. It was still preparation but to express myself in a non-physical, totally mental arena.

The best students of the Sammies were often-times small in stature and less developed physically than my athletic combatants. But what a difference in introspective thinking. Interests were as varied as

Lester Berke
Gerald Cogan
Allan Freeman
Louis Handler

Philip Berk
Ted Cohn
Sanford Friedman
Irwin Horwitz

Bod Berke
Richard Corngold
Jerry Gartman
Don Jacobs

Stuart Bisk
Fredric Dunn
Jules Gerber
Norman Jacobs

Sigma Alpha Mu

1953

The Jews who took me Inn

were the number of individuals. Guys with names like Jerry Fox and Ted Wallace and Ben Kagen and Bob Memel and Dave Waller and Norm Jacobs and Dave Meyers and Stu Wallace and Art Kahn were my academic role models (not all you guys!). These comrades yelled and screamed for every basket and victory we experienced in basketball. I am moved to say, Thank you, Fellows, even the ones I did not mention. A special thanks to "Stu," who gave me daily unscheduled, unlimited use of his brand new sky-blue Lincoln Continental convertible. I'll never forget the day five Jewish boys and I were cruising down 103rd Street in the middle of Watts. I was driving with the top down, waving to the people I knew who waved back and treated us as though we were visiting political dignitaries of fame. None of my passengers had ever been in this predominately African American section of town. Acculturation was working two ways now as we stopped and filled up on Pop's hot dogs. We all agreed that Pop's prepared the best dogs we had ever experienced.

Many nights we went to the Village Delicatessen for pecan pie and ice cream or corned beef on rye. I introduced my mayonnaise addiction to them by adding thousand island dressing to my pastrami sandwich. I never thought about it at that time but most of the restaurants in Westwood had never had Black skinned sit-down customers in their shops before. So we experienced cross-cultural food tastes. For the first time, I was introduced to the concepts of tipping someone and splitting the check six ways. Even the idea of going to a restaurant with a bunch of guys who had done this all their lives, but were sensitive enough to not make me feel uncomfortable, was all new and very special to me.

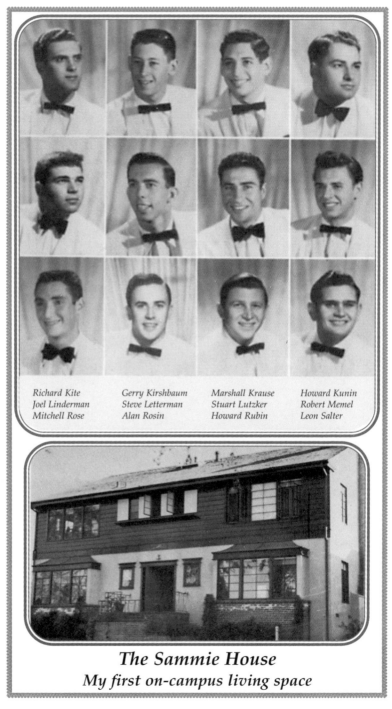

Richard Kite   Gerry Kirshbaum   Marshall Krause   Howard Kunin
Joel Linderman   Steve Letterman   Stuart Lutzker   Robert Memel
Mitchell Rose   Alan Rosin   Howard Rubin   Leon Salter

The Sammie House
My first on-campus living space

My Sammie brothers invited me anywhere they were going. I was introduced to upper middle class White society in Beverly Hills, Westwood, Brentwood and Santa Monica by the young men who took me in. They told me that they were less impressed with my All-American basketball status than they were with my humility. We went to the movies at theatres in West Los Angeles and Beverly Hills, or we took dates to the Olympic Drive-In Theatre on Olympic at Sepulveda. We often stopped at Truman's Drive-In on the southeast corner of Wilshire Boulevard and Westwood Boulevard in Stu's car with the top down or McFarlane's Drive-In for hamburgers on Pico Boulevard.

We ate Kosher food daily at the fraternity house prepared by Helen, the house's African American culinary genius. She loved me and treated me like her son. Helen is remembered as a dear person, friend and cook. Breakfast, lunch and dinner, she prepared hot gourmet meals. NCAA rules barred me from participating in any organized off-season league play my freshman year. I gained 45 pounds of Helen's love. I learned to pray and even led prayer in Hebrew as we thanked God together before every meal. It was just like being at home, except we spoke Hebrew. Forgetting that I was the only one covered with Black skin, the boys eventually changed my name to Willie Naullsberger and told me in the comfort of humor that they thought they had detected a developing hook in my nose.

The big negative that I experienced was having no privacy. I slept in the freshman dormitory space with three small drawers but no closets for all of my clothes. The double-decked bunk beds were the same type as those in my home in the projects of San Pedro. I was grateful but always looking to improve my living condition to that of the thousands of non-athletes I interfaced with daily. So after two and a half years I moved out of the Sammie house.

In retrospect, my soul was unsettled at every turn for I was a reputed STAR who had no home where I could rest and meditate during the time when the sun was blessing the other side of the planet. NCAA rules allowed a student athlete to work but we were only allowed to earn a minimum number of dollars. I was reduced to being a street hustler to survive and lived out of my car, by choice, some of the time. I could have gone back home to Watts, but I refused! Nobody asked me, "How are you doing, Willie?" The Athletic Department's advisor said that all the other athletes were doing just fine and suggested that I could and should do a better job of managing my money. What money, I thought in silence. Besides, I made enough money but no one would rent to me. A teammate's grandmother – Grandmother Nickerson, whom I dearly loved – invited me into her home in a newly integrating section of West Los Angeles for a period during my senior year. Her husband and family founded the Golden State Life Insurance Company. My soul was quieted for that productive part of my college career. I knew Grandma wished me well.

I give this background to enlighten both Black and White skinned readers of the challenges of Black students at UCLA during the 1950s. It is a worse condition to be stereotyped as a non-class of people because of color than to be considered second class because of economic conditions. Class is a term intruded upon some to make others conscious of a perceived arbitrary distinction between identifiable groups of people. Praise God my mom's **Lesson** let me know that "God looks only at the heart of all people."

On the day I scored a school record 39 points against the University of California Berkeley during my last year of eligibility, we clinched the conference championship. I did not know where I was going to sleep that night. My dad had mentioned several times that I was welcome back home any time I wanted to sleep there, but I was hesitant to do that. From Westwood back to Watts – even though the distance of 15 miles or so was the same – was a mountain higher than I could travail at that time. The system, in the silence of its firm commitment to the status quo, attempted to put me back in my place. The more successful my reputation became before UCLA fans, the more amazed I was to experience how callous the community residents' resolve was to keep separate Black skin from White skin. Coach Wooden never broached the subject and I stewed in my mother's teaching that mental overload is controlled when I count my blessings in silence and patience. "Just work hard to do your best and let God be God, William."

When my eligibility was used up, my Jewish brothers and I departed in our different directions to fulfill our dreams and aspirations. For the next ten years I lived mostly on the east coast and saw very little of any of the ΣAM crowd. Upon returning to the west coast after retirement from professional basketball, some of our paths crossed. I rented my Beverly Hills business office from Big Ralph Shapiro, a student I had met at the ZBT house when visiting Johnny Moore during my first few days at

UCLA. He became a friend indeed who taught me to think big and be honorable in business. Many of the Sammies were raising their families and developing their legal, medical and other professional entrepreneurial careers in this area. Bob Memel comes to mind as the leader in the development of the International House of Pancakes Restaurants. What now emerges from my heart is a poem to meditate upon about my Jewish friends of old.

Ralph Shapiro
Zeta Beta Tau

ZBT empathically housed Johnny Moore's Black skin, a pioneering act of grace in the 1950s at UCLA

Sam Silber
ΣAM President

who came to Coach's office to offer me housing

Norm Jacobs
1955

My SAMMIE friend was an athlete. I don't know if any of the basketball or football players could have pulled off this leaping feat.

Did You Ever Ponder?

Did You Ever Ponder,
maybe to grow fonder,
what it would be like
being a Jew?
Forever linked to a calling
that few people knew?
Why the hatred?
Can it be traced back
to a history intact?

"Leave your country, your people,
and your household, too. . . "
Abram, you "GO to the land
I will show to you.
I will make you into a great nation
and I will bless you," too;
"I will make your name great.
I will bless those who bless you,
whoever curses you I will curse,
and through you, all the people
of the earth, I will come to nurse."

So Abram left Ur,
as he was instructed,
continuing from Haran
where his father was interrupted.
Taking his nephew Lot
he set out from Haran
and arrived in Canaan,
where the Jews began!

Again, the Lord said to Abram,
"Lift up your eyes and see . . . ."
north, south, east and west –
all this land I give to thee.
And, "to your Offspring Forever"
means every Jew ever born
is linked through inheritance
to shoulder the scorn
of such a great blessing
to bless others to be
the fruit of God's Promise
from the Seed of SEED Tree.

So, I Encourage You To Ponder
about way back yonder
as you try to understand
how the Faith of one man
could possibly be a link
to how the anti-Semites think.
Even today, when a Jew
with his prosperity in full view
openly declares by name
his historically founded claim
that God committed His Word
to never leave nor forsake
those Jews who by nature partake
of God's blessings to His Namesake.
Brother Paul gave insight, that
some branches are broken off
and wild olive shoots grafted in,
making it clear not to scoff
boasting over those branches' sin

because graftees don't support
    THE ROOT
THE ROOT forever supports
    THE RECRUIT.
Finally, we are told, that Salvation
for the world is from the Jews
Eternal life in Christ
for anyone to choose
where circumcision is more than
merely outward and physical,
but, is Circumcision of the heart
by The Spirit, where no code is critical.

Jesus Christ came, as same
Jewish Messiah in name, did proclaim,
establishing forever the Line to toe
God through Him by which to grow.

Amen!

"GRACIOUS SAKES ALIVE!"

Dreams of Surrogacy

Surrogacy
is Substituting one failed teacher for
    the other
Gaining A Role Model for me to
    uncover
where to run for refuge and cover
when abandoned by a parental lover
for protection of my mind to recover
God's Purpose in my soul to discover

I became more and more curious about who Coach Wooden is as I interfaced with him frequently during my freshman year. His presence in my life represented a positive, strong role model of a father figure that I never had. In my mind, my dad and I had officially dismissed each other the day I left for UCLA. My cautious – naïve – desire was for Coach to spiritually engage me with the closeness of a father – in that image of surrogacy. Never having experienced love from a man before, I was cautiously looking for a break in his fortified, strictly business position. I soon sensed that there was a boundary between player and coach and that the most I could hope for from him was a fair assessment of my talent.

I moaned to myself in my immaturity that all of the White skinned players had family near, whether

For - Willie Naulls & Family.
Love. John & Nell Wooden
4-4-2001

Coach and Mrs. Wooden left indelible imprints in my mind of what a husband-wife love relationship could be – yea, should be.

fraternity brothers or actual geographic closeness to their homes. My father closed the door to me in finality after our mutual declaration that it was time for me to fly solo from his nest. Of course, it wasn't Coach's responsibility to soothe my growing inner pain and my need for love from a father; nevertheless I was out there without a settled living condition. I was totally committed to the segregated and isolated world of UCLA basketball and student body. How could Coach fulfill my need for a loving father role model and give wholly to his responsibilities as UCLA Basketball Coach, husband to Mrs. Wooden and father to their children? Nevertheless, I thought him to be the living walking of my mom's teaching's talking.

I am liberated to write openly about my college days' innermost thoughts and desires after all these years of in-house storage. Picture a stray black puppy trying to nestle up to a mother cat in the middle of her litter of all white kittens. My mother placed me on the road to not think of myself as a skin color, but I was reminded daily of what I perceived Coach and all of the other White folks thought of me. They didn't think about me. Everywhere I walked in Westwood Village or on campus, people recognized me as the new basketball jock on campus and few – mostly females – engaged me in thoughtful conversation. Then they were off to their sorority or fraternity houses or apartments. Hundreds, even thousands, of smiling White faces, daily passing in review.

Mom's presence emerged as I drove from the Hummels' home toward UCLA the morning after my last confrontation with my father. My thoughts drifted back to Dallas, sitting beside her in a pew in the sanctuary of Greater El Bethel Baptist Church. Her arm around me, her hand stroking the side of my seven year old temple, she sang along with the rest of the congregation.

> Nobody knows the trouble I've seen
> Nobody knows my sorrow.
> Nobody knows the trouble I've seen
> Nobody knows but Jesus
> Nobody knows the trouble I've seen
> Glory, Hallelujah!

Her voice interrupted, "Stop feeling sorry for yourself, William, and count your blessings. Therein lies your direction – to trust God for guidance. Let go of the wrongs you think people have done to you. Forgive them and rid yourself of the heavy weight of judging others for the decisions they have made. That's God's job alone! Just make sure you, William, are trusting in God and are not acting like the people you are judging."

> Is my Focus only on Me
> and not to relieve
> the challenge of the present
> God's Word to retrieve?

The first day on campus I discovered the Athletic Department's changed attitude toward me. While recruiting, they eagerly provided me with a parking pass when I visited the campus. Once I was a registered student, the University's policies were in place and my attitude needed an adjustment, first about the parking issue.

In defiance, I parked as close as I could get to the

center of the athletes' world in forbidden parking spaces between Kerckhoff Hall and the Men's Gym. Most of the athletes didn't have a parking problem because they lived on campus or parking was provided, especially for the football players. On some days I was fortunate to find parking on Westwood Boulevard near the Men's Gym, but most of the time I literally let my car park itself.

After accumulating several citations, the Chief of Campus Police brought "my attitude" to the attention of Coach Wooden and Athletic Director Wilbur Johns. On my way to class one bright sunny day, I stopped at the kiosk located in the middle of Westwood Boulevard, two blocks south of Sunset Boulevard. The parking official there said, "A representative of Coach Wooden just left here and wants you to contact Coach as soon as possible. I believe it has something to do with parking violations." I thanked him. My conscience kicked in and I drove all the way around the campus via Westwood Boulevard, north to Sunset Boulevard, east to Hilgard Avenue, and south to the unpaved area used for unknown student parking. This area was the future location of the UCLA Law School and the furthest anyone had to park from the athletic facilities. I walked to my class and afterward all the way back across campus to Coach's office. All this walking wasn't mentioned during negotiations or in the fine print of my scholarship.

There he sat, waiting for me with his arms crossed and this "gracious sakes alive" look on his face. He said, "Well, you have certainly made yourself known on campus; at least your car is known by every campus police officer on staff. No parking zones mean **No Parking!** Now, I want you to march

UCLA Men's Gym, where my car parked itself on many occasions

over to the traffic violations department and pay every one of those tickets, and let's not have to discuss this again, Willie. You are smarter than what your early reputation around here is indicating."

"OK, Coach, I apologize, but I don't have any place to park."

"Welcome to student campus life here at UCLA. You are a student athlete and do not deserve any special parking privileges."

Talk about a pin in my "fullness of myself" balloon. Mom's Lesson: "Pride goes before destruction, a haughty spirit before a fall" (Proverbs 16:18). I knew better and it was good that Coach reminded me of my upbringing. But what about the verbal promises? I assumed parking was included in *"No Problema, Willie, No Problema!"*

"OK, Coach," were my last words as I pivoted through his office door. He didn't even offer to pay for my tickets, so I had to dig into my stash to clean up my record. When I went to bring current my obligation, I had amassed 15 parking citations, costing me a total of $47.00: $2.00 for each ticket plus late fees. That was a lot of money for me to pay out, but I was reminded of a valuable Lesson my mom taught me: "If you break the law, you will have to pay the penalty." Coach also taught me a lesson: "Don't pay for someone else's crime that he should pay for himself. It takes away his dignity." I thought to myself, *Coach is not giving me my propers.*

This act of defiance was a new thing for me. My mind swirled as Mom's words reminded me, "William, don't get too full of yourself." What in the world did she mean, too full of myself? Her words continued to rise up in my mind as important in evaluating a man's character: humble, honest, faithful, trustworthy, dependable, accountable, earnest and doing unto others as I would have them do unto me. The weight of this thinking was getting heavier and more uncomfortable every day. I knew what was right and I was severely challenged to always do what my mother taught me to be right before God and in my best interest. How long, I thought, before I'm rid of her rigid adherence to God's final answer?

I sensed relief when I moved west from Watts to Westwood, but soon I heard Mom's voice emerge through Coach John Wooden's demand that I shape up and be the developing man that he had recruited. I sensed that I had let him down for the first of what would be many times during our long association.

The day I was busted for my ingenious book reimbursement scheme, I was again summoned to Coach's office. He sat behind his desk with that intellectual scowl of disappointment on his brow, staring across at me. The big bad warden, Athletic Director Wilbur Johns, was standing erect just behind Coach's left shoulder, his shoulders squared off and hands folded behind his back. He appeared stoic – God Almighty, with Lord Wooden sitting at his right hand. "Willie," came a voice from the echo chamber in the back of Mr. Johns' head, "the game is up. You will pay back every dime that you embezzled from this University."

Coach tilted his head and let it all out: "GRACIOUS SAKES ALIVE, WILLIE. What are you thinking? I know your mom and dad didn't raise you to act like this."

I sensed a callousness over my conscience as I left Coach's office. I had no shame, only embarrassment and remorse that I had been caught and had to

Wilbur Johns

Athletic Director
1947 - 1963

A man who knew coaches, Wilbur Johns looked beyond the west coast. He sought out and hired both John Wooden for UCLA Basketball and Red Sanders for UCLA Football

pay the money back. In retrospect, I now know that once I deviated from the **Lessons** Mom taught me, a veil over my spiritual eyes gave me an illusion of grandeur. It's difficult to explain away doing wrong when I knew to do right. I even wanted to do what was right in my thoughts to honor Mom's teaching. But – getting all I could get for what I perceived I brought to the table at UCLA was a dark side which I had never experienced before. I blamed racism, lack of living quarters, everybody and everything else – but myself. It was me: my choices were steering me up the wrong road.

Coach's words to me were final and stern. "Gracious sakes alive, Willie. I know your parents didn't raise you this way. Look at yourself in the mirror and I don't think you'll see the young man your parents raised you to be." I was learning I wasn't that special, that I would have to obey the

Coach Wooden

"Gracious Sakes Alive!"

rules or get into serious trouble. I remember vividly sensing an opportunity to grow up. No one threatened kicking me out of school. There was an unspoken forgiveness from Mr. Johns and Coach Wooden. UCLA was evolving into a great place to grow up – through another, and another, and yet another chance. I know! You're saying to yourself, Coaches let great athletes get away with murder. Not so at UCLA, my friend. They saw something in me; a sparkle from the Lord's light in me. And I kept coming back to UCLA's watering hole to drink and prepare to do it better through another chance. Finally I got it and was graduated twenty-six years after the day I had first enrolled at UCLA.

Mom's **Lesson** popped up on the screen of my mind: "William, remember that if you don't work for what you get, it's not worth having. Especially money. You can't love money and do things God's Way at the same time. If you do what God tells you to do, you will be all right. The love of money will cause you to sell your soul to the devil. The love of money is the root of all evil. Earn all the money you want to by the sweat of your mental and physical brow. That is the abundance that God will give you as He grants you the desires of your heart."

Ma, you've got to stop resting so heavily on my mind.

Before the fall of the racial divide in Westwood, California – and before I came under the influence of the teachings of Coach John Wooden at UCLA – my mother laid the foundation for my expected behavior. Another comparison reveals the thread of similarity between the words of Mom and those of Coach Wooden. As she quoted from Scripture, "There's nothing new under the sun." (Ecclesiastes 1:9)

Willie the Student

*A UCLA journalist wanted a photo of me
in the library.*

Mom: "Do it right the first time, or you will have to lick the cat over again."

Coach: "If you don't have time to do it right, when will you have time to do it over?"

I thought I was rid of Mom's **Lessons'** lectures, but at every turn she "phoenixed" before me. That very insecure period of my freshman year was bombarded with her soft recurring whisper. I did not want to hear her voice – but I heard. I was trained up to be a "good boy" but I yearned to be bad and have some fun and experience life. I was tired of the restrictions of the mental boundaries of parental control, so I rebelled loud and clear. The UCLA Basketball Players' rules of engagement set down by our combat general, John R. Wooden, introduced his boundaries of expected behavior. Too many people giving me orders. I walked around campus talking to myself like a babbling idiot. Finally – I decided that it was in my best interest to play the Wooden Games and see where that led me.

God does have a sense of humor. From under the loving hand of Bettie Arlene Naulls to the demanding and structured world of "the man," Coach John R. Wooden – I had come a long way from Dallas. This man called Coach had an aura of "welcome to my world and here are the rules and regulations by which we will engage each other: You are a student first here at UCLA who partici-pates in our basketball program. It's up to you, Willie, to make the most of the opportunities that your talent presents you." I remembered that college coach from long ago who had introduced me to the word "scholarship" when I was in the ninth grade. Well, I got one, scholarship that is, to the biggest university in our town and I had a lot of growing up to do to demonstrate that I was deserving of UCLA's confidence in me.

Levitation's View:
Looking at Me through Your Eyes

Looking at me through your eyes
raises the question on which doubt
    thrives
Can I ever know without a shadow of
    doubt
that you really do care what I am all
    about?
Skin to skin – White looking – Black
    back at you
Did you ever want to know me enough
    a friendship to pursue?
An equal footing sealed in your desire
    to know my heart
Looking at Me through Your Eyes were
    we doomed from the start?
Was our potential lessened by the
    playing of game by game
until my value to all involved did erode
    to reflect the same?
That you really didn't think to know my
    depth, growing more tactful every
    year
until, I am – an ex-DOG – dimly lit in
    your mirror rear

Integration in the Melanin Game
Black and White
– and –
Black and Wannabe White

UCLA was more than basketball, but no White student campus organization recruited me. As a young man of 17 years, I was accustomed to assessing the facts of any situation and spontaneously making decisions that I thought were in my selfish and best interest. Unselfishness, I thought, was White folk idealism. Unselfishness amid racism? An oxymoron?

My mind shifted back to that alleyway behind our home on Church Street in Dallas. The face of that young White boy who wasn't allowed to play with me because his mother *and* my mother thought the White men-folk wouldn't approve haunted me for a spell during that period. I wondered where he was and what his life had developed into in the previous nine years. Might he be a freshman here at UCLA? Then it hit me right in my heart. I didn't even know his name. I pondered during my private quiet time: *Does anyone here at UCLA want to know me – and the spirit behind my voice? Do they really think of me?* I meditated further. *Are all freshmen students in the same dilemma of sensed meaninglessness? Some stare as though they have never seen an African American up close. What about the Black skinned classmates I left behind in segregated Dallas? Would any qualify to enter UCLA? The major universities in Texas didn't want them.*

In class together, White skinned girls, who

appeared to be less intimidated by me than White skinned boys, often commented on the smoothness of my skin after I gave them permission to touch me, like I was the Rare Rock of God's placement. A smile from my heart surfaced when, at the end of a lecture, a young, wide-eyed brunette smiled at me and said, "Aren't you Willie Naulls?"

I whispered, "Yes, I am."

"You don't know me, but your team beat our school in the City Tournament. I didn't like you very much then. I'm glad we're on the same team now." She smiled as she departed with a touch and grasp of my wrist.

I smiled, "Goodbye."

The smile from my heart was triggered from memories of Mom's words: "People stare at you, William, because you are tall, dark and very good looking." I never took her seriously but the thought of her words was always uplifting. When I was most upset in my mind's eye, I often sensed her voice's whisper as she read to me from the Holy Bible:

"William: 'Peacemakers who sow in peace raise a harvest of righteousness' (James 3:18)."

Again, I thought, is Coach Wooden the living walking of my mom's **Lessons**' talking?

More words of Wisdom from Mom came immediately to mind. "You are never alone, William. God is right there with you every minute of every day. Listen to Him. Don't pay attention to other voices who offer only temporary fixes and not long range solutions that will benefit you." Her voice was getting faint and questions from other voices came more frequently; specifically, *Why don't I have a special place to stay? Every one of the White players has convenient living accommodations provided for them. So – why not me?*

The more I thought about the situation, the more I isolated myself inside to resist an overt outburst against that institution which I knew so well, racism. But – a voice screamed from Mom's **Lessons**:

> . . . Obedience to God is required
> Judgment by skin color is not of Him
>   inspired . . . .
> "Grow up, William."

Wow! Could it be that I was "letting what's around to see / entice [me] to become whom God didn't create [me] to be?" *No way*, I thought. *I'll never be a racist!* Her voice continued:

> Use your mind to stand against wrong's
>   wooing
> Think before you act in unwise doing.

I emphatically declared out loud, "I AM NOT A RACIST NOR WILL I EVER BE!" But – the other voice continued: *Can a Black skinned man be a racist? You haven't attempted to suppress or suffocate anyone!* In the freedom to mentally counter-punch in the arena of UCLA Basketball, I declared to myself and to that *other voice*, "I will make my stand – within the rules of the game." Mama often reminded me, "After all is said and done, you're better off in any condition imposed on you at UCLA than any other Black man in the White man's world. William, God does provide for His children."

What did a Christian look like in the 1950s at UCLA? I was impressed from afar with the overt

Donn Moomaw

Donn was my first great All-American college football hero.

Jim Brown

This Christian gentleman was UCLA's All-American tackle, Jim Brown.

identifying with Christ by Donn Moomaw, an All-American linebacker for the Bruin Football team my freshman year. There were other football players and probably some basketball players who were officially associated with the Campus Crusade for Christ, but I don't remember any of the groups inviting me to a meeting at school or in their churches or homes. The body of Christ was divided along color lines at UCLA in the 1950s, mirroring our society. Maybe I was running so fast away from Christian identification that even the fastest athlete couldn't catch me. They never did, but I knew who they were: Johnny Moore, Bob Davenport, Terry Debay, Jimmy Decker, Jim Brown. Yeah, I knew who the Christian guys were and I respected the fact that they were vocal about the Jesus my mom taught me was the answer to my every problem. The common characteristics of these young men were a twinkling smile of confidence and a meek and quiet spirit. Most of all I was impressed that among the leaders of UCLA's number one NCAA football team in America, meekness in Christ equaled controlled power.

I privately searched for fellowship with some of the new faces I encountered on the sprawling campus. A non-athlete who became a close freshman associate was John Considine. I suspected he was a member of Campus Crusade for Christ. He had a beautiful girlfriend who drove a powder blue convertible Mercedes Benz with a royal blue soft top. She had blue eyes to match her car and the two of them made a powerful impact on me. They were the first two people to engage me personally in conversation with what appeared to be genuine interest. After classes we often drove along Sunset

Boulevard, the northern boundary of campus, with the top down. On this day we headed east toward the adjoining town, Beverly Hills. Sitting in the front seat next to his girlfriend, with John insisting that he sit in the back seat to give me more leg room, expanded my thinking about confidence in oneself. I thought to myself, *John is a* bad *White boy to not be threatened by me in this situation.* His girl was "fine" in the vernacular of the streets of any day, of any time.

We drove east for a couple of miles to Whittier Boulevard just across the border into Beverly Hills, took a right turn past what I perceived to be a mansion or two and then right into the driveway of John's parents' home. This was the largest home I had ever seen. The landscaping looked like my vision of the Garden of Eden of Biblical fame. We headed for the front entrance. An African American housekeeper met us at the door with a beautiful smile on her face. "Hello, John. Who's this big handsome son of mine with you?" They all laughed and my smile directly in her face let her know that I was overjoyed. She grabbed my arm and ushered me out of the entryway and into another area through large paneled wood doors. John's mother and younger brother, Timmy, greeted me with the brightest happy faces that I would ever record in my memory. I thought, *Thanks, I needed that.*

We had a surprise Welcome-Willie-to-UCLA lunch. They never suspected that it meant a lot to me. I'm sure they didn't have a clue what I was sensing that day, but Timmy – later to be the famous Mickey Mouse Club Mousketeer idol – and John communicated with me about their lives and asked me questions that got beyond my physical

Hollywood was in the House

that state taxpayers built named the
University of California at Los Angeles, UCLA

Debbie Reynolds
at a 1955 Dance

Marilyn Monroe
at Junior Prom in 1952

Joe E. Brown

Joe E. Brown's
leading of the UCLA
yell was dearly loved
by UCLA fans.

characteristics of height, skin color, etc. They were gracious people who took me on an unplanned, slowly evolving tour through their home. John, Timmy, their parents and guests had individual rooms to think, to develop confidence in their privacy. John's mom invited me to come and stay with them any time I was lonely and in need of a friend to communicate with. Were they being courteous or serious? I never had time to find out. This one year hiatus from basketball was to be my last freedom of choice for many years. Even though I saw John on campus passing on the upward or downward trail between classes, we never planned anything social because of BASKETBALL.

In hindsight, I never took the Considines up on their offer because of my upbringing, but their attitude toward me resembled the work of the Spirit Mom taught me to look for in folks God would put in my path. The Spirit of genuine interest added some gravel to the mix cementing in the sandy based foundation which insecurity was forming inside. John and I spent less and less time together as our schedules were controlled by demanding pursuits, but my soul remembers his kind and gentle heart when I needed a demonstration of God's Spirit the most. John expressed his rearing by yielding to God's Spirit which was the real Campus Crusade for Christ at UCLA, at least for Willie Naulls. He was the man that God sent to say hello to me. I am inspired to call him and thank him after all these years. I have seen him in many movies and have always wanted to know of his family's where-abouts and health. The Spirit behind my voice is wishing them well.

UCLA African American women were called Negroes when I visited the campus in the spring semester of 1952. Of the thousands of members of the student body, the male and female descendants of the seed planting from Africa made up less than one percent. The enrollment numbers hadn't changed much by the fall semester and slowly, day by day, I nodded hello to each of these articulate and friendly Black skinned coeds. I didn't know what to say that would interest them in conversation, so I just listened and smiled. These young ladies were as well dressed as any group on campus. The intoxicating fragrance of their perfume stimulated me to get closer, but these well raised sisters didn't play that game. So we made small talk and they invited me to their parties in town in an area called the west side of Los Angeles. At these parties were every shade of Black cascading through Brown into an increasing influence of White skin covering.

These beautiful and chosen women and men were the storm troopers in the war of integration as were the Black athletes, but their challenge focused on academics – the mind. Their decision to take a stand in competition's quest to be each woman's or man's individually prepared best, academically and socially, was a foundational stand for Black people. They appeared determined to make a difference with their lives through gathering the knowledge stored in the minds of UCLA's great professors. I had never seen such a wide variety of beautiful African American women. Even when I mustered up enough courage to make a lame move toward one of these ladies, their response was profound and expressive: "WILLIE – PLE-E-E-E-ASE!" They were preparing to share what they learned at UCLA with

A
K
A

A
l
p
h
a

K
a
p
p
a

A
l
p
h
a

s
i
s
t
e
r
s

Rudell Slay

Sylvia Griggs

Mary Ann Buford

Gail Rucker

Nira Hardon

Vivian Credille

AKA Alpha Kappa Alpha sisters

Jacqueline Miles

Sheila Montgomery

Janice Williams

Effeta Davis

Marianne Fulcher

Vivian Robinson

Δ
Σ
Θ

D
e
l
t
a

S
i
g
m
a

T
h
e
t
a

s
i
s
t
e
r
s

Patronella Ross

Barbara Tyson

Virgie Brown

Alora Anderson

Mildred Hamilton

Gloria McPherson

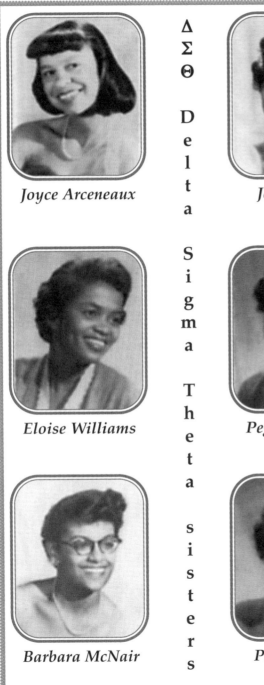

Δ
Σ
Θ

D
e
l
t
a

S
i
g
m
a

T
h
e
t
a

s
i
s
t
e
r
s

Joyce Arceneaux

Joan Crisp

Eloise Williams

Peggy Wooley

Barbara McNair

Pat Flowers

Vivian Robinson

advanced the cause of freedom in the academic arena, even as we Black skinned athletes fought for space and time on the field and on the court.

Member of the Student Legislative Council and the Project India team of 1953 Future Ph.D.

Diane Watson

From UCLA coed to attorney to California State Senator to United States Congresswoman, she has represented us well.

Yvonne Watson Braithwaite Burke

From UCLA coed to attorney to the California State Legislature to the United States Congress to the Los Angeles County Board of Supervisors she has represented us well.

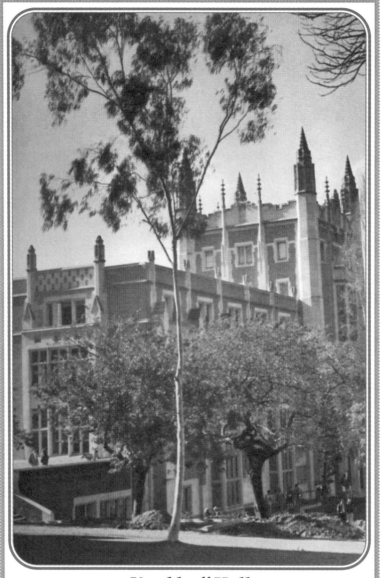

Kerckhoff Hall

Scene of the mid-afternoon Black Summits and passing in view of the most beautiful California girls

the community of Black skinned people who were left behind. The unequal conditions intruded upon those left behind included a silence from the Voice of hope.

On the lawn in front of Kerckhoff Hall I met new faces, many of them African American. On a gorgeous October day nearing my 18th birthday, a beautiful young lady walked up to me, extended her hand and said, "My name is Yvonne. Welcome to UCLA, and if there is anything I can do to assist you in adjusting to our campus, I'd be happy to do so." Another African American, who introduced herself as Vivian, joined us and, without provocation and in the ease of self confidence, they proceeded to draw a grid on a blank page, write in my scheduled classes in the appropriate time slots during the week, and even pencil in suggested amounts of study time for each class. These students really impressed me. They were so organized, intelligent, comfortable and confident in themselves. I had never met girls of my race who were this open and in my face to share their knowledge with me. Later I met African American pre-med students Herbie and David with Gerald Strange, several football players, and Halvor, Rick and Nira who were future lawyers. I sensed that they were supportive of my decision to accept an athletic scholarship to UCLA.

An illumination beset me that Black skinned men and women I was getting to know were as serious about academics as I was about athletics. They were there daily to remind me that I was a student first, who participated in basketball, just as Coach Wooden had said earlier. My athletic career at UCLA demanded increasing amounts of my prime time. The mental inflation of success filtered my desire to study and learn to exercise my mind with zeal equal to that I gave to the development of my physical skills in basketball. The results were predictable: Basketball = All-American; Academics = completion of two and one-half years of courses in four years of University attendance with a "C" grade point average in an "undecided" major. No UCLA degree earned during my athletic career there. But – I would be back. As it turns out, my mother didn't raise no fool.

A bespectacled African American student approached me one day as I walked daydreaming up the steps of Kerckhoff Hall. He extended his hand and said, "Hello, Willie Naulls. My name is Bill Thayer and I'm a member of an on-campus fraternity. We are entering the campus intramural competition and would like you to consider playing for our team." After Coach Wooden had authorized my participation, I arrived at our first practice and met Leon McCarty, Harold Garrison, Willie Collins, Dave Williams and Gerald Strange. Gerald, a pre-med student who influenced my decision to attend UCLA, was President of this group, the only African American fraternal group on campus. We defeated all comers in the name of ΚΑΨ (Kappa Alpha Psi) and cemented in the minds of all who observed the competition the compelling conformity to segregation at UCLA.

This was my first experience of playing with all Black men and they were very pleased with the results that we dramatically imposed on every Greek organization during our Championship sweep. After all was over, the University was unshaken, again settling into its Segregation Status Quo. Black skinned folk were kept in their place.

Top Row:
De Witt Adams
Willie Collins
Ulysses Griggs
Jay Johnson

Second Row:
Harold Morgan
William Naulls
Reginald Pierson
David Reed

Third Row:
Leon McCarty
Don Mims
John Moore

Fourth Row:
Gerald Strange
William Thayer

Kappa Alpha Psi
Fraternity
1953

These Ambassadors of Los Angeles' Black skinned population represented the most committed and academically prepared in our country. They developed into educators, medical doctors, PhD's, lawyers, bankers, business professionals, administrators, professional athletes, coaches.

From segregated Dallas to integrated San Pedro, back to segregated UCLA. Which direction was I headed? Away from or back to attitudinal racial and color poles? Through my eyes alone, I saw Black skin pitted against White skin. We Black skinned folk won the intramural battle but I suspected that our efforts did very little to impact the War on Racism. Ponder this: In one of America's most liberal and respected educational institutions, the combatants of intramural sports teams in the 1950s were categorized thusly:

White-skinned non-Jews
White-skinned Jews } vs. Black skin

We had come a long way . . . but, as that slogan concludes, baby, we sure had a long way to go. But God's movement comes through the patience of faith's eyes.

I was told that very few African Americans played in intramural sports at UCLA before this championship team. As Mom would optimistically say, "Praise God for His progress." My analysis is that in open integrated competition men honor superior talent, and mental barriers which separate are lowered to accommodate the exceptional performer. The *Daily Bruin* included accounts of our team's exploits and the campus newspaper's articles propelled me into many spontaneous new relationships. Integration's growth spilled over into the other's bucket and we were mixing.

My childhood exposure to a Black-skin-only environment was interrupted during my ninth year when my family moved from Dallas to San Pedro. Most of the African American students at UCLA during my athletic eligibility had matriculated from

Whitney Arceneaux
Football

Popular football player whose pleasant smile welcomed me on campus.

Doug Peters
Football

Great athlete and very effective, perhaps our most powerful fullback. A gentleman and powerful representative of the Black skin race.

Pete O'Garro
Football

The most talented who never got his chance to be an All-American.

Tom Adams
Football

Another great football playing end in the midst of a great team.

Edison Griffin
Football

A great unleashed talent who demonstrated composure and self control.

Esker Harris
Football

Fierce competitor and quick. All-American.

Don Shinnick
Football

My high school teammate in baseball. Held the interception record for linebackers in the NFL with the World Champion Baltimore Colts.

Ike Jones
Football

Very popular brother with all people. Great football player who became a motion picture star. Recently honored for pioneering work in film production and direction.

Chuck Holloway
Football & Track

*A great football and track
athlete.
In today's football world,
he would be a
successful professional*

Hardiman Cureton
Football

*Hall of Fame offense and defense.
The best among great football
players at UCLA during my
undergraduate career. Fierce
competitor honored
as Captain by his peers.*

Rommie Loudd
Football

*All-American. Great speed,
hands and power. Played both
ways and pioneered the tradition
of great end play at UCLA.*

Clarence Norris
Football

*An introspective, highly
respected student athlete,
Clarence worked out of himself
what God had put in.*

Dr. Milt Davis
Football & Track

Revolutionized thinking about Black athletes at UCLA. Became Milton Davis, Ph.D. in Biology. Played both offense and defense in football. In track, a sprinter. Long-time All-Pro professional football player with the Baltimore Colts and a highly respected professional scout.

Dr. James D. Collins
Football

J. D. Collins had to be all about business because of his pre-med commitment. Developed into a medical doctor specializing in radiology.

Sam Brown
Football

Came to UCLA as "FIRST DOWN" and left as "Sam TOUCHDOWN Brown" Recognized nationally as the most dangerous offensive threat in football in the USA during his career at UCLA. History has not recorded his greatness nor his impact on UCLA's opponents.

All-Americans Jim Salsbury, Jack Ellena and Bob Davenport

These were Godly men of FCA who were role models for all of us to emulate

ucla	67 –	0	san diego navy
ucla	32 –	7	kansas
ucla	12 –	7	maryland
ucla	21 –	20	washington
ucla	72 –	0	stanford
ucla	61 –	0	oregon state
ucla	27 –	6	california
ucla	41 –	0	oregon
ucla	34 –	0	southern california

UCLA's undefeated #1 National Championship 1954 football team was unable to make a repeat appearance in the Rose Bowl because of the conference rules.

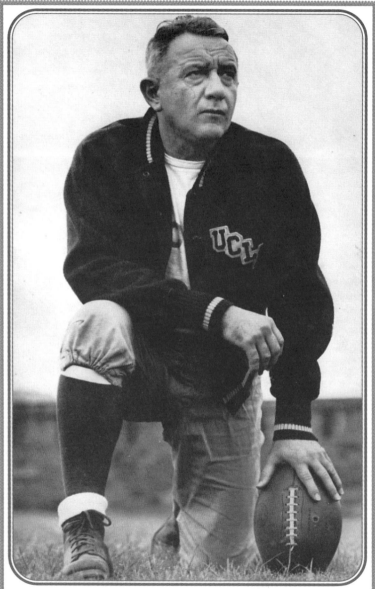

Coach Henry R. "Red" Sanders

The greatest UCLA football coach.
Approached me about coming out to play football.
I told him that my body was four years removed from the
toughness required to compete effectively in football.

Rafer Johnson
Track & Basketball

*The most dedicated
of any of us.
Student Body President
Olympic Decathlon Champion*

Dr. Rodney Richards
Track & Field

*Led UCLA to respectability as a
foundational consistent winner
in the 100 and 220 yard sprints.
A big heart, to win the prize.
Medical doctor.*

Nick Dyer
Track & Field

*NCAA High Jump first-place
finish earned UCLA its first
NCAA Championship.
Very pleasant and kind spirit.*

Halvor Miller
Track & Field

*The Conference Champion
contributed to UCLA's first
NCAA Track & Field
Championship.
Successful attorney.*

Ulysses S. Griggs

One of the really good people to evolve in my life's history. Always positive, always optimistic, always dependable. A good man who served all of us in his sphere of influence. Always wished me well.

Rafer Johnson and Coach Craig Dixon

Rafer's personal trainer was Coach Dixon, who was himself a national champion in the hurdles.

What Rafer and I never realized until a conversation recently is that he and I both lived in the Oak Cliff section of Dallas, Texas, on opposite sides of the grave-yard, until we were nine years old and our fathers relocated our families to California.

George Brown & Coach Wooden
at a 1952 rally

I wonder if the great George Brown remembers the words of wisdom that the great John Wooden employed this night.

George Brown • UCLA Track
1952

This man, George Brown, was the greatest long-jumper in the history of high school Track & Field at Jordan High School. He set many high school and collegiate records. I personally saw George jump OUT of the pit in high school – clearly over 27 1/2 feet. The officials put their heads together and disallowed the jump because it was beyond the end of the pit. How many times in integrated sports in the 1950s did officials confer to deny Black skin accomplishments? Should he be in UCLA's Athletic Hall of Fame?

Dr. Russ Ellis
Track & Field

The lion-heart charged from the rear to overtake every opponent without any fear. Driven to academic excellence, his Ph.D. did declare the quality of his soul for future Black skinned students to bear

Russ Ellis • UCLA Track

1955

all-African-American high school environments. As I looked into the eyes and heard the voices from the hearts of these young men and women who thought of me as *brother Willie*, I was impressed to know more about them and their family environments. Isn't that a trip? Socialization became environment-intensive. I was a Black young man integrating into a familiar White environment and into unfamiliar Black environmental socialization.

The White students at UCLA were Jews and non-Jews from various all White neighborhoods. Most of the Black students were from the African American communities of Los Angeles. Until we moved to Watts during my senior year in high school, I lived in the projects of integrated San Pedro. We were all being acculturated into the UCLA culture. Black folk and White folk started paying some dues, giving diversity a *blending* stir for other generations to peruse.

There were more than two worlds I found myself integrating into. In the system of this world, I was taught to submit to the authority of governments. There was the forced rule of the White skin over every other skin coloring. What I discovered at UCLA was that Black skin became categories of gradation separated by Black hue domination. In the minds of some insecure Black folk, the further their skin covering's color was from the dominant Black gene, the closer they were to being accepted by White folk. Thus some assumed a superiority complex in their recessive gene prominence.

My new Black *brothers and sisters* taught me some terms of endearment I had never heard before. "High Yeller," "Red Bone," "Brown Skin," "Dark

Skin," "Mariney," "Creole" – all categorical stereo-
types referring to the gradation of pigmentation of
the Black skinned category of students at UCLA.
This was new to me so I shut down and sponged
up their tongue flapping to understand this new
vocabulary. But it was a Black thing put on Black
people whose disgruntled minds succumbed to
generational brainwashing influenced "educational
materials" such as that written by a colonial
plantation owner in his Willie Lynch Letter, "How to
Train a Slave." That same spirit which influenced
the minds of White people and influenced every
Black person to look upon himself as a degree of
melanin mixture on the campus of UCLA is still
alive today. There I was, Willie Naulls, the soon to
be proclaimed "Big Black Whale" of Westwood by
White folk even as some Black folk looked upon me
as a field nigger because of the strong melanin in my
skin.

On the campus of UCLA, we were all products
of earned integration. Discovering that my Black
brothers and sisters were divided as the White
brainwasher had prophesied centuries ago stunned
me. Hook, line and sinker, deep into the soul's
jugular where it meets the spirit, that prophecy had
sunk into my racial group's perception of self. Some
were pitiful echoes of that "Lynch Letter." They
were blinded in the light that pitted browning bright
against damn near White. At a moment of high
reverie I stood in my tracks to be me, from the inside
out, not who they saw me to be, but ME – for I AM
WHAT I AM.

I AM What I AM

When you see,
> Do you really see Me?
And, when you hear,
> Do you really hear through to Me?
Way inside what you see as Me
> Is a voice to be seen as Me and heard
> as Me.
I am more than what you see or hear Me
> to be.
For I am!
More than perception
> And conception
Of what appears to Be,
I am Me!
Hear Me and know that I am
> Real -
And see Me through seeing -
> Not through sense alone,
> > But, by Faith, as Being.
Real, eternal Me.
I am, more than sight alone,
> But Seeing -
See through to Me, for
I AM what I AM In Christ
> Who Empowers Me
> To be Me.
I AM what I AM.
". . . by the grace of God,
I AM what I AM,
and His grace to me
was not without effect."
I AM what I AM!

Most African Americans lived off campus in the city. I received more and more invitations to exclusively African American social events and was further educated on how deeply these categories of skin coloring were enforced. In Westwood and at UCLA, the majority of White skinned folk thought of all of us as Niggers. But to each other, we were being encouraged by an invisible historical plantation mind set to assign more prestige to "High Yellers" than to "Dark Skin." What a mental trip that took my mind on. We as a race/skin color were running away from the African Blackness which gave us our root identity in the world. But God has said, "The Lord does not look at the things man looks at. Man looks at the outward appearance, but the Lord looks at the heart" (I Samuel 16:7). Could it be that some Black skinned people hate the color BLACK on themselves so much that they want to create a separation between themselves and the next level of too much melanin? Where had I come to? My soul was confused. Should I feel horror or sadness or rage? There was a sifting effect reverberating through the Black folks' agenda. Various degrees of melanin were running through the sieve – the smallest doses first, followed by increasingly heavier doses – with those first sifted shouting to the darker tones, *Stay in your place!*

My mom's **Lessons** made living in the midst of the extremes of segregation and on the front lines of introducing integration more understandable. I decided to obey the rules imposed by men who Power Brokered society. God would intrude His will when He prepared a man to lead His agenda for change.

Coach John Wooden had the attitude required to

The Sparksmen

Taft introduced me to a new social scene in Los Angeles, where beauty and well-bred young women were abounding. Morrie became captain of my social ship. The men here are Maxie Floyd, Donald Thompson, Leonard Pollard, Willie Naulls and Morrie Taft. The first and third women from the left are Barbara Weaver and Gina Limeau. I don't recall the other names. "The Sparksmen" was our socially dawned name and partying was our game. All in the name of good clean fun.

be God's man. Basketball was a medium used by God to influence men to integrate this country. Every morning I got up to face another day of basketball experiences with hope in my heart to find fellowship and give it in return. By this time in my life I had trained myself to listen to hear sincerity from another person's heart to mine. I was eager to find a like kind openness to share inner thoughts and ambitions with another and to hear their vulnerabilities and dreams. But every so often, when I least expected it, an incident involving one of the varied color strongholds would remind me of what others perceived to be my place at UCLA.

*Bobby Pounds was the first player covered with
Black skin I saw in a UCLA uniform.
I often thought at the time that he pioneered
it all in Coach's reign and no one recorded his
voice or cared enough to seek out his pain.*

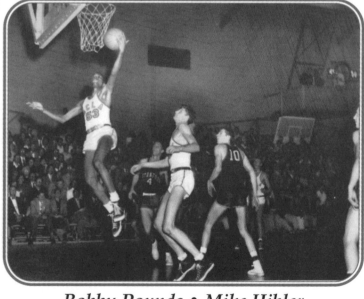

Bobby Pounds • Mike Hibler
1952

Retrospective's Testimony

I never smoked dope
I never got high
Most of the girls thought me
a square kind of a guy
No experience in sex
or hatred toward man
Only tempted in the classroom
to get away with all I can
Didn't steal money or property
of the faculty or students in my sphere
Nor did I respond in like kind
to the hatred White folks made clear
Lowered expectations of one another
made it easier to pass in review
up and down the hills on life's conveyor
    belt
as status quo won approval at the Spring
    Sing's minstrel review
Not a word from my Coach
when I thought to demand his attention
He continued his stand on man's
    philosophy
and not the issue of students' blackened
    white faces to mention
Politically it was thought better to shut
    down and listen
and to let God be God in any situation
than to expect that a just cause
would be supported by every one of His
    creation

UCLA Blackens Its Face for Spring Sing

Over a year after Brown v. Board of Education, in the fall of 1955, 14 year old Emmett Till's mutilated body was displayed in an open casket at his funeral, forcing the nation to observe White skinned hostile brutality directed at Black skinned people. At UCLA, these fraternity men and sorority women won their competitions in successive years (1954 and 1955) for their portrayal of their disdain for Black skinned people. My soul was confused by Coach Wooden's silence as we began preparation for my senior year in the fall of 1955. Should I have protested and walked away from college basketball? My conclusion was that the Black skinned race's battle is on every front. All fallen sacrifices open up doors that must be entered by the souls that God has prepared to walk through them. What say you on this issue of university-sanctioned degradation of my race? How would you have reacted to these, my fellow Bruins, all White but covered with Black paint to disrespectfully mimic my race with no apparent consciousness of our humanity?

Kappa Delta Sorority Women, Spring Sing Winners, 1955

Sigma Alpha Epsilon Fraternity Men, Spring Sing Winners, 1954

On Pride in Color
Christ Is My Seal of Approval

Black skin covering is beautiful
and White skin covering is too
when love is shared as unto a brother
in the Spirit – given one to the other

Featured in the world
color is a plot to divide
perversion of satanic origin
reducing separation by hide
Judging by genetic selection
is not of the Master's plan
but – the transformation of our minds
in God's purpose on which to STAND

Mind games' intentions, as serious as
        death,
affect entire races of people as destiny's
        theft
But, what did my mom tell me, that did
        stop the flow
of everything that the enemy would
        viciously throw?
Hear her words:

A principal fallacy of the world's "peace
    of mind" view
which did promote my social accultura-
    tion coup –
is that those who thought they had "peace
    of mind"
hadn't sought the Peace of God – to find
that Ignorance has spread around the
    world,
through judging people first by color
encumbering every boy and girl.
What a deceiver is the Pride in Color!

Belief in Christ Jesus is my Seal of
    approval
according to John Six 25 through 29
Not my parents' work of blending
but Faith, of Him, in me, to refine.

In Immaturity's Freedom
I Raced Toward Death

With all four windows down in my lowered, dual-piped, two-toned Chevy, I cruised the streets of Watts and East Los Angeles on my way back to Westwood and the UCLA campus early in my sophomore year. My mom had convinced me to return home for the weekend to celebrate my 19th birthday with our family. She hooked my mind up to visions of her Hall-of-Fame Chocolate Cake. It was five layers high with a half inch of delicious chocolate between each layer. I invited a couple of teammates over to share the goodies. Johnny Moore couldn't believe the food my mother prepared, but the cake was the featured and enshrined item of the day. The boys took huge slices home with them as they left me to spend the night with family.

After helping clean up after the feast, I had a powerful catching up session with Mom. At about five in the afternoon, we decided that it would be OK with her if I did not stay over night, so I headed west. I drove through the Beverlywood area just south of Beverly Hills and turned west off of Beverwil Drive onto Pico Boulevard. At a stop light east of Fox Studio's back lot a hot rod pulled up next to me and raced his engine to get my ego's attention. I raced my engine in retort, and when the signal light flashed from red to green, we were off in a dash toward the Pacific Ocean. As we crossed in front of the entrance to Twentieth Century Fox Studios at Motor Avenue, our speed neared 90 miles per hour. In my rear view mirror I thought I saw a police car making a U-turn and my first instinct was to hit my brakes and attempt to go north on Beverly Glen toward campus. But, alas, my reaction speed had slowed down to only 75. The hot rod had evidently spotted the patrol car also for he quickly got over into the right lane. He cut off another driver who found himself innocently between us.

By the time we were in the right lane, driving below the 35-miles-per-hour limit, the officer pulled all three of us over and demanded that we get out of our cars. Obviously irritated, he began to lecture all three of us about how dumb racing up and down Pico Boulevard on a Sunday evening was. In silence my chin was resting on the middle of my chest and I heard this voice saying to me, "Gracious sakes alive, Willie, what have you done now? First parking tickets. Now you're a bona fide illegal race car driver. Gracious sakes alive, Willie!" Coach's voice had replaced Mom's. Did this mean that I had matured or was my mind tripping?

The officer's direct question snapped me out of my trance. "Which one of you was not racing? We were passed by only two cars." I raised my head and looked, for the first time, into the eyes of the innocent victim. His exasperated expression was relieved when I told the officer that mine was the second car. My honesty didn't stop the officer's release on me. He gave hot rod and me a tongue lashing and said, "I'm of a mind to take you both to jail for endangering the citizens of this community." He continued to write the ticket. "Where do you live? Is this address on your driver's license correct? Is this your current address?"

Inside my mind, I sensed a gleam of hope. I said very confidently, "I'm on Coach Wooden's basketball team at UCLA and I live on campus. I'm on my way back to school now."

There was a hesitation. The officer stopped writing the citation, looked into my eyes and asked, "Does Coach Wooden know that you drive with such recklessness?"

"Coach will take care of this," I let out before I could stop myself. The words out of my mouth confirmed that at least one of the drivers was living out the aforementioned stupidity.

Staring at me in disbelief, the officer said, "Well, let me give him something to take care of." He wrote me a citation for 95 mph in a 35 mph zone. He said, "If you don't show up in court, I will personally come pick your tall cocky A– – up AND put you in jail! And your coach too!" He pushed the ticket into my chest and said, "Now, get on out of here before I change my mind and take you to jail NOW."

The five mile trip back to the fraternity house was the most miserable of my life. This officer had threatened to put me and my coach in jail, for a legitimate reason, excessive speeding – and endangering of the lives of others – at 95 miles per hour. I compounded the violation by wrongfully including Coach Wooden. What was I to do?

At practice on Monday I broached the situation with Assistant Coach Doug Sale, in the hope that he would introduce the subject to Coach Wooden. "How fast did you say you were going, Willie? Practice doesn't start for another 40 minutes, so go get the ticket. I want to see it." I was back in 20 minutes and stood before Coach Sale as his eyes almost popped out of his head.

The next day Coach summoned me to his office

You guessed it: "Gracious sakes alive, Willie. I don't know if we can keep you out of prison this time or not. What were you thinking racing up and down our streets like that. You could have killed yourself or someone else. You must become more responsible or you are going to get yourself into more serious trouble. Now, you are going to face a judge and pay your fine. I'll have nothing to do with it. You got yourself into this mess and you'd better throw yourself on the mercy of the court. You may still go to jail unless you can pay your penalty. GRACIOUS SAKES ALIVE, WILLIE! GRACIOUS SAKES ALIVE!"

The judge, on the day of my appearance before him, asked me, "Have you ever been to jail before, Willie?"

"No, sir, Your Honor, I have never been to jail before."

He said, "How's the basketball team going to be this year?"

"This is my first year and I'm not sure of my role yet, sir."

He said, in a very stern voice, "Coach Wooden is a fine man and I know he must be very disappointed in your actions. Because this is your first time here, and because I respect your coach, I'm going to give you the benefit of the doubt. I want you to remember this experience. I won't take your license away but don't let me see your face in my courtroom again. Is there anyone here to vouch for you?"

"Yes, sir, there is Coach's assistant, Coach Sale." The judge nodded to Coach Sale, who nodded back to him.

"I'm going to follow your career, young man. I

expect you to be more responsible than you've demonstrated thus far. Will you be more responsible and obey the law?"

I was surprised that tears of shame flowed freely from my eyes, down onto the tip of my nose, meeting under my chin. I was so embarrassed as I said, "Yes, sir, I will." I was ashamed, not so much because of my tears in front of all those people in the courtroom, but because Mom's Lessons had taught me better behavior.

> . . . don't let what's around to see
> entice you to become whom God didn't
>   create you to be
> Use your mind to stand against wrong's
>   wooing
> Think before you act in unwise doing

After I paid the ONE HUNDRED AND FORTY-SEVEN DOLLAR FINE out of my stash, I went back to UCLA with the gorilla of violating the law off my back. At practice I saw Coaches Sale and Wooden conferring and could imagine their exchange. Reflecting back to when I was learning how to drive, Dad, as my instructor, told me that there was a difference between watching and doing the driving. Being responsible enough to be trusted with an automobile was his "big deal." Now I didn't need his approval or anyone else's. What would I do with my independence? The **Lesson** that my mother stressed as she encouraged me to ponder my choices: "Be responsible to yourself, William, when you are a man."

I'm So Sorr-e-e

I'm So Sorr-e-e!
What a pitiful use
of words used as an excuse
of an insensitive abuse
calling for an exonerating truce
calculating to reduce
the penalty for one's crime!
What a pitiful use
Sorr-e-e does induce

Sorr-e-e
used to mean regret
a sympathetic and paltry upset
for one's action by mistake
to understand the amends to make

But – not so today
In whining decline
a selfishness of me and mine
I'm sorry has evolved
in Sorr-e-e's resolve
to lighten the sentence
in a scripted repentance
that's worldly staged
which has Godly folk enraged
'cause Justice is imprisoned
What a pitiful use
is Sorr-e-e's excuse!

I'm So Sorr-e-e
When you've stolen their money
or abused his wife
causing a ripple effect
changing the rest of her life?
influencing their mental strife –
Sorr-e-e?

I'm So-o-o-o Sorr-e-e!
Translates: she's copping a plea
hoping that the judgment of her sentence
will not mirror her crime's severity
How selfish the cry
how hollow the tears
and the manufactured fears
preferring imprisonment for years
prolonging, maybe for ever,
Justice, to fit the crime – to sever
satan's work, so clever
to use Sorr-e-e as a scheme
for shattering what was a dream

We have been brainwashed
to "just give 'em another chance"
so that Sorr-e-e agenda continues to
	advance
Now our neighborhoods are filling
with non-repentant criminals' plea
who scream and are set free,
acting out – I'm So-o-o-o-o Sorr-e-e

My First Year in Prime Time

Shortly after my 19th birthday, I was given an opportunity to work to earn a starting berth on Coach Wooden's Bruin basketball team. Coach summoned me to his office for a visit which prompted my decision to try out for the varsity team. He sat across from me behind his modest desk in his very modest office. As we made small talk about what I had learned during my freshman year, I scanned the walls filled with action photos of past and current players. My eyes settled on a three or four part blow-up of a player launching a shot from the defensive team's free throw line that traveled three-fourths of the court into UCLA's basket for one of Coach's early victories. My mind wandered a bit, into "That should have been me!!" Yeah . . . so I dreamed of being a hero. Haven't you?

Coach drew me back into our meeting's purpose, offering, "How would you like to forego your freshman year and play for the varsity?" Even though I was in the worst shape of my young athletic life due to idleness, I really never considered the long range consequences of my decision. I blurted out, "OK, Coach." I had not been looking forward to that first year of mandatory freshman play. It was my option, as he informed me, because I had entered UCLA during the second semester of the two-semester system of that time.

As I approached the new challenge of competing against what were the White world's best athletes who ended up on the UCLA Men's Gym Basketball Court, I was confident that the inner city

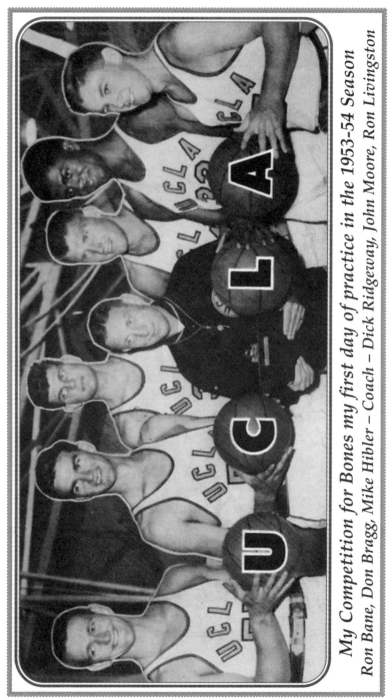

My Competition for Bones my first day of practice in the 1953-54 Season
Ron Bane, Don Bragg, Mike Hibler – Coach – Dick Ridgeway, John Moore, Ron Livingston

playgrounds of south central Los Angeles had prepared me well.

From a very young age in San Pedro, I had a sense of physical superiority in the integrated athletic world. A strengthening lesson occurred at 13 years of age when I was denied a position on San Pedro's local American Legion baseball team by a coach who would be honored in its Hall of Fame after his death at a ripe old age. As faith would have it, that same authority was humbled in his desire to win when he sent some of my schoolmates on his team to hustle me in succeeding years. We are all familiar with the Proverb that "pride comes before the fall." My ego enjoyed saying "NO" to his appeal for my talent. His players, some of whom I considered friends, were well known to me as competitive athletes in other sports. All of these young White boys had fallen victim to my God given talent in baseball, football and basketball. All of them knew that the coach had not allowed me to try out for his team the previous year because of the color of my skin. They knew I was a better player than any of them.

My mother's **Lessons** shored me up for my run in the '50s. But what about all those young boys and their parents who looked on and even enjoyed the false sense of security that comes with having positions set aside for them? They were mentally damaged by the coach's evil decisions. Over the next few years, several became self-destructive through substance abuse. White affirmative action in sports had the same effect as Black impeding action. If each competitor doesn't earn a place through fair and open competition, maximum expression can never be achieved.

The Bruin Six

Livingston, Hibler, Bragg – Coach – Ridgeway, Bane, Moore

*returning together as a unit in the fall of 1953
Each one my foe – for dem bones*

That preparation impacted me as I eyeballed the group of athletes that first day of tryouts for positions and playing time on what I considered to be this White man's team. Johnny Moore was the one other player of color as I looked calmly into the uneasy, cocky clusters of eyes, summing up, one by one, each by position, thinking to myself, *I'm not sitting on this coach's bench! Just give me an equal chance to live out my passions and dreams.* After the whistle blew, my focus shifted toward the voice of the man who led us, Coach John R. Wooden.

Interesting observation to note that day: Three clusters of young men were designated: the white jerseys, the blue jerseys, and the third group who would sub in for one of these two groups of colors. We were not grouped by skin color, but by different-ly colored scrimmage jerseys awarded for previous years' performance. We were all fighting to be the coach's chosen representatives of our University, to wear the Blue and Gold. I was in the third group waiting for anyone of the ten on the court to stumble. I was mentally and physically ready to move in on any lame or inferior teammate.

I wondered, who is this man who had told me with a firm but endearing hand shake and genuine eye contact, "Willie, I'd like you to come to UCLA and play for our team. UCLA is a good place to get an education. You have great potential and I think you could develop into a very fine basketball player. You can determine whether you will make a positive contribution to our society." Who is this man? Emerging from my insecurity, a voice questioned my decision to attend UCLA rather than UC Berkeley. But I had given my word to UCLA and I intended to honor it. "A good name is more

desirable than great riches [Proverbs 22:1]." Why
did I have such a thought? Who was attempting to
influence me?

> . . . . The direction of one's life is
>   compassed in choices,
>   couched in heart's recesses, influenced
>   by voices. . . .

I must stress that, after leaving my home in
Watts to attend UCLA in Westwood, I did very little
of what I had been taught. At 17 years of age and
thereafter, I used everything I thought of to my
advantage. People who thought of me as a color, an
adjective, were at a disadvantage. I thought I was a
Man when I stepped out from that world of
absolute parental control. Mom had been a Godly
parent, preparing me spiritually and mentally for
that moment. Now I had the luxury and privilege of
choice, to do it Mom's way or my way. I chose my
way. Led by the overwhelming rush to gratify my
mind/body connection, I let it rule. I submitted
myself to my new coach's authority for I had no
other choice in his arena. But I was the authority in
the rest of my time. With UCLA perfectly located
seven miles from the Pacific Ocean to the west, five
miles from Beverly Hills to the east, and one block
from Bel Air to the north, separated by famous
Sunset Boulevard which ends on the shores of the
Pacific, I was ready for prime time encounters.

Occasionally I thought to myself, *These folk got
me cubby-holed. This Westwood is segregated just like
Texas. They want to use me up and spit me out where
they think I belong. I was taught to pray for the White
man who would abuse me. Is John Wooden any different*

after court hours? He has never invited me to his home. Maybe he doesn't trust me around his family.

When I was young, I sometimes questioned Mom's unwavering faith in me. How could she be so confident that I could ever live out her high standard? Even as I stood in the back row of practice mentally prepared to launch my college basketball career, I was living out her faith, patiently pursuing, to ripen on her tree. She wanted me to work out of myself what she saw God had given me so I could benefit myself, my family, my community and all whom He put in my path. God didn't look upon me as a genetic mix, which is obvious to see, but rather upon the spirit and heart in me as real through Christ to be. In other words, God is the Spirit who searches the inward parts of my belly, and He knew the prideful error of my conviction, to choose to be a Man at 17 years, to "DO IT," in the words of that popular song, "MY WAY."

Competitive sports are not a series of fun and games but a series of opportunities to participate in games that college and professional folk take very seriously. Like me in the back row that first day of practice. As I said, I didn't choose UCLA because I thought I would sit on the bench. I came to play ball – NOW! I was taught that "no weapon formed against me would prevail" (Isaiah 54:17). I didn't even know what the Scripture meant then; but upon reflecting, in the midst of that day's stronghold of institutional racism, I was ready at all times to be at my best at any time, especially and specifically in basketball. I was ready to work out of myself a first team UCLA Bruin Basketball position. My goal was to attain the standard of **Competitive Greatness** on John Wooden's Pyramid of evaluating success in his

THREE SOPHOMORES TO WATCH!

Polytechnic High School   San Pedro High School   University High School

Morrie Taft   *Willie Naulls*   *Denny Miller*

athletes.

During the second or third week of weekday practices, I was promoted from the last man on the team to the second team of blue jersey clad gladiators, which played against the first team, consisting mostly of upperclassmen. As mentioned previously, I was in the worst condition of my athletic life. Undergirded by my attitude to persistently invoke my will on whoever had the ball or was in my way to get the ball off the backboards or attempted to stop me from putting the ball in the basket, I gave my all. Then it happened: a break in the ranks. One of the first-teamers in white took his best shot and intentionally nailed me in the pit of my stomach with his elbow.

As I pivoted away from his blow to turn my face from his rage, my mom's words influenced my decision, to choose to wage a physical war with this first-stringer or decide to ignore the demon who influenced his behavior. He was clearly outside the rules of basketball. The rules of ghetto street ball I know, but Mom's voice came forth: "To respond to another's attack on you is like pouring gasoline on a fire." She had recorded these words into me long before this encounter. I doubled over a bit, took a few steps away, out of bounds, under the backboard that I lived to control, and took some deep short breaths. The practice was stilled and the man at the head of the court observed and appraised his warriors' responses to battle conditions. Should I go the macho route and retaliate? After a few steps away from the ring, I chose to take my space on the court again. My position was on defense, against the first team. After his whistle summoned our attention, Coach's words resounded in my ears and ricocheted off the beams of the Old Men's Gym ceiling, "We are here to develop as a team in basketball, and basketball is a game of finesse with rules and regulations, and we all must, and we will, play by those rules – and in self control and determination and become the best we can be." After we were all ordered to get a drink of water, he blew his whistle and we were off and running again, competing, as quick as the sound of it, for playing time.

My mom's prayers, that I would receive open minded evaluation from those in authority, were answered by her faith in God that day through Coach John Wooden. During a practice soon thereafter, my enthusiastically industrious presence was rewarded. Coach said, "Willie, you run with the first team today. Take off that [blue] jersey." In a moment of high inner triumph and satisfaction, I walked over to the other side of the court. My innermost self screamed, *YEAH.* In the midst of it I thought, *Now I have to really go to work.* I reaffirmed my commitment to play at my best at all times. Did I ever let Coach down? You bet I did, but never consciously. During my trek I gave my all to win, to be called by him "competitively great" in basketball at UCLA. Where I failed Coach, and especially Mom, was in the realm of my off-court choices.

A central part of being a successful person in my mom's eyes and a successful person and great Bruin in Coach's eyes was that a young man should live a life of Godly character. I did not know at the time that Coach was pulling from the same Source of one-liners as Mom. It is evident to me now that God was always there, everywhere, within and throughout my life, from the beginning. Retrospectively questioning myself, have I ever been at my best? Can we ever be at our best knowing that being at one's best requires absolute obedience to God's will to be done through our choices? According to Scripture we humans have a "whole duty" before God:

> *Now all has been heard;*
> *here is the conclusion of the matter:*
> *Fear God and keep his commandments,*
> *for this is the whole duty of man.*
> *Ecclesiastes 12:13*

Diversity's Birthing

Imprisonment inside self-imposed hang-ups is not a White or Black thing. Every time I attempted playing the race card in my thoughts, a loud booming voice reverberated, "Count your blessings." From Dallas to San Pedro to Watts to Westwood Village was a hop-skip-and-jump that only God could giant step. Every step of the way was preparing me to be well able to take the land wherever I found myself at any given moment on any given day.

The autumn air was brisk on my face as I walked toward a class across the promenade between UCLA's four original buildings up on the hill. Faintly I thought I heard a familiar melody coming through the giant open double doors of Royce Hall. It sounded like . . . I drew nearer. It was Beethoven's *Moonlight Sonata*. The musical notes heightened as I crossed the threshold into the main lobby of this historic building. There was a lone student poised and erect, performing as before a capacity auditorium, not acknowledging that I was the only other person there.

A faint voice whispered, "Get up and go to class" as the gonging bells registered the beginning of the hour. I sat through three complete practice sessions before the pianist realized that she had an audience. She stared at me for an extended moment, then asked if she could be of any assistance to me. I told her that she already had been by performing my favorite of the few classical pieces I remembered from tenth grade music appreciation.

"What are the others?" she smiled through

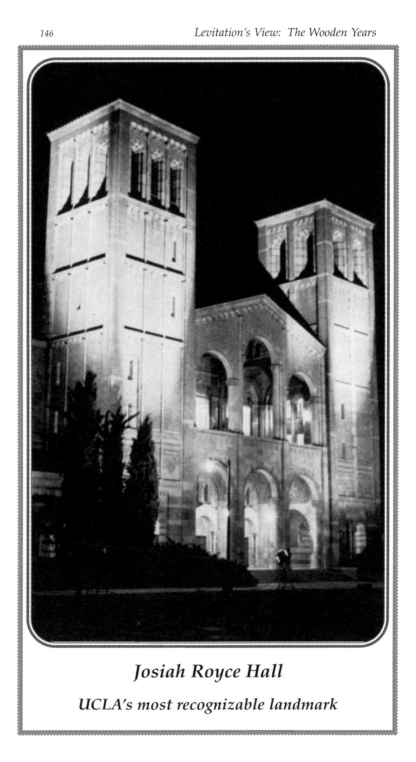

Josiah Royce Hall

UCLA's most recognizable landmark

friendly lips.

"Brahms's *Lullaby*, Grieg's *Piano Concerto* and *Fur Elise* by Beethoven. "

"If you have time, I'll practice those on you."

I moved closer into a different vantage point. Her long pale fingers massaged the keys as her body reacted in rhythm with the composer's intent, but in her own uniqueness of movement. When she closed down the Power in *Fur Elise*, I glanced down at my watch and realized that not only had I missed my class but it was nearing practice time. The thought of being late for hoop-ball practice was not only as serious as it got, but it poured water on the igniting sparks. I thanked her for the special performance and was on my way up the aisle toward the exit.

She caught up and asked if I were in a hurry. I told her about the seriousness of being late for basketball practice. "I'll walk over with you, if you don't mind." As we neared the walk down to UCLA's lower campus, her face moved closer as she put her arm around mine and smiled, "People don't just happen to meet for no reason, do they? You were drawn to the music that I was practicing at the same time you walked by the open door? What can we read into that?"

Before I could answer, I sensed a presence behind us to my left just before we approached the famous Janss Steps. It was Coach Wooden. I stopped as he crossed his arms and brought forth his intellectual scowl. "Hello, Coach, this is . . . ." I had never asked her name. "Mary Lee," she offered. With a bright smile, she extended her hand.

He shook the young lady's hand and said, "It's nice meeting you, miss. See you in practice, Willie." He smiled and was on his way.

White and Black students and faculty repeated double-takes on us over the next several months as we stood laughing and getting to know each other. We delved into exploring in conversation what our new friendship would bring. In later months she revealed to me that I was the first Black skinned person she had ever talked to or touched. She was raised in the Bel Air/Brentwood private school community which she said had never experienced integration. Two years later, when my star was the brightest in Coach's eye, this young student's father came up to me after a late season victory and apologized for forbidding his Presbyterian daughter from seeing me again. I forgave him with little fanfare because she had never told me about his attitude. She was two years ahead of me in school and had graduated and, I believe, gone on to Harvard's School of Medicine.

Many years later, on the night the Boston Celtics won their seventh and my first World Championship, there she was with a handsome young man whom she introduced to me as her professor husband. Alongside them were their three beautiful children. "Do you remember me, Willie? Do you remember me playing *Moonlight Sonata* several times a week for you in Royce Hall?" Her smile lit me up as it had so many years before. Then there she was, up and around my neck in glee and honor of knowing each other at UCLA.

My thoughts raced under the inspiration of her face against my neck and in the fullness and freedom of her form against mine. My senses were in shock as she pulled away to look into my eyes and exhaled, "Willie, Willie, my dear Willie. How have you been all these years? I've followed your career in the papers, but how have you been?" She grasped me again, like Melanie's embrace around the neck of her beloved Ashley as he limped back up the main road to Tara in defeat. That kind of a hug – with a Grace Kelly sparkle and hair style, but an Olivia de Haviland sincerity in her eyes. My body's makeup exploded to the brink of control, and I knew I had to rid myself of her grip. At that potentially embarrassing moment she knew to release and draw back, turning away with, "This is my husband and family, Willie." His handshake was firm and confident. A sensed desire to embrace him as a brother was broken as their three children meandered over to say hello to *Uncle Willie*.

I looked into her eyes and saw a genuine interest in me, past the demands my body put on my mind to read something more into her openness than was there. "I'm just fine," came forth as I released her from the strength of my force around her, and hers around me, looking, and moving toward her family.

Her husband said, "She's talked about you every day since I met her and you were my only competition for all our years of courting and marriage." I assured him that he had nothing to worry about all those years because she had never even hinted that I was a mountain for any of her male friends to climb over. My date for this game was a beautiful and brilliant African American senior student at one of the colleges there in Boston. She spent most of the evening talking to Mary Lee's husband as we filled in the years with speculative blanks of "What ifs."

Lest you get a confused impression of what transpired between us in college, she informed me that night with sparkles in her eyes that her husband knew she was still a virgin when she married him. She made him respect her and all the other men she had special relationships with before him, by telling him the truth about each during their normal conversation. En route to the end of our reunion, my date told all of us that she had fallen in love – platonically, of course - with Mary Lee's man. "You've got a good man here, Mary Lee – for a White boy, that is." We laughed in the spontaneity of accepted humor.

The purpose of this story is to share this young woman whom I introduced to Coach Wooden the first day that I met her. She was dramatically impacted by her perception of Coach's obvious displeasure in seeing us walking around campus arm in arm. Her parents had emphatically let her know that no one had ever witnessed such a scene before at UCLA. I told her that I was almost late for practice that first day and Coach knew that fact when she met his expression. She had mistaken his brow's source and had embraced a negative impression of him all those years. Her parents were UCLA Basketball boosters and had talked to Coach about me. Mary Lee's final non-judgmental word was, "Everybody back then was against what I thought in my heart about you, Willie."

I looked deep into her sparkling eyes and said, pointing toward her family, "They were right, weren't they?" We got up and walked toward the others, arm in arm, as we had done that first day of *Moonlight Sonata*.

A song title emerged from inside as I attempted to understand the emotions surfacing that night: *A Man Ain't Supposed to Cry*. All of a sudden I felt a sense of a wasted life, drifting further from – never to reach – the shores of my real purpose. Why had Mary Lee emerged at the very point when the dulling thrill of victory in sports suggested the futility I sensed at the apex of a robotical championship season. *The Thrill Was Gone* but my mind and body would continue to play their games for two more curtain-call championship seasons.

During private time apart from the others, Mary Lee questioned my inner state. "What if we could run away from responsibilities to stop the momentum of being on the proper track of others? Would you run in the other direction toward your purpose, Willie? Could you muster up enough strength for both of us?" Then she brandished that Kelly girl smile.

"Mary Lee, you always were a dreamer of 'faith-ing away' the invisible societal boundaries which separated us."

"Fantasies can form visions which mature into realities, can't they, Willie?"

I am sure that we were both comforted to know that we were not compelled to make decisions as our noses bumped to toast our suspicion about the other. Her eldest son interrupted the flow of this truth forum asking, "May I sit on your lap, Uncle Willie?"

Lesson: God orchestrated this spiritual reunion between two unlikely souls from diverse backgrounds out of His family of chosen children at UCLA. Mary Lee and I had committed back then to save ourselves for the one person God would send as our life long partner in marriage. The thought of her understated and mature presence pressured me to look upon our college days relationship with spiritual sensitivity. The physical desires which were on occasion so overwhelmingly present were always beneath my desire for true friendship. She appeared especially empathic when I shared with her that my virginity lasted through college. What's the **Lesson**? Most people in the UCLA environment during my college days thought of me as a hound dog – not the virgin I was. As Mama taught me, "You can't judge a book by its cover!" Social pressure never saw through to uncover – Mary Lee to Willie – only a spiritual lover.

During my college days there were caravans of young White men from UCLA and the African American contingent of college males from all over Los Angeles who routinely made the trek to Tijuana, Mexico, to buy some relief. I thought they were crazy and refused to subject my body and soul to such a depraved state. *Can't buy love*, I thought. Thank God that He gave us the freedom to make choices and He alone is our judge. I didn't make that bad choice – but I made many others which violated my mother's teaching. For the record, Coach, when I left your care I was a virgin. Not necessarily of my choice – but greatly influenced by Mom's VOICE.

Love's Seed

Love is in the Pit of it all
the Seed – where the residue is so thick
fermenting Passion in the heart to beat
    quick
blending goodness in every season
causing people to smile in everlasting
    reason
Love's Seed is the Pit of it all
there the enemy forgives generational
    foes
forestalling current and future woes
Love's Seed is the Pit of it all

Loneliness is such a lamenting affair
a burden which Love comes to eternally
    bear
'cause Love's Seed is the Pit of it all
raising hope out of nothing left over
promoting faith instead of a four-leaf
    clover
Love's Seed is the Pit of it all
Are you cast down in the depth of a fall?
Jesus is the Sage One on call
Love is in the Pit of it all
Omniscience giving you His Power to be
    – as He
His Hand to grab when no one else can
    see
how you can get out of the mess you're in
Love is the only Victor over where you've
    been

Hearken unto His Voice – He's calling
cleanse your heart of all your forestalling
Seek to rid the weight of the burden
of your daily march toward death certain
Love's Seed is in the Pit of it all
The Seed where the residue is so thick
fermenting Passion in the heart to beat
    quick
blending goodness in every season
causing people to smile in everlasting
    reason
Love's Seed is the Pit of it all

Are you wondering where he is tonight?
Promised he'd never be out of your sight?
BUT -- your glow became a dimming
    bright
thinking – he's chasing lust's brilliant
    light
moth in purpose was his soul's delight
Love is the Pit of it all
The Seed where residue is so thick
fermenting Passion in the heart to beat
    quick
blending goodness is every season
causing people to smile in everlasting
    reason
Love's Seed is the Pit of it all
Jesus will heal you if you heed to His Call
Love's Seed is the Pit of it all

Do you still call me Nigger
when you react in earnest reflex
a condition – after all these years of
         context
and in spite of an active affirmative fix
after liberal based actions and contrived
         mix
am I to know – in summation of full
         review
that I still remain Nigger to you?
Love's Seed is the Pit of it all
Jesus will heal you if you heed to His call

Do you still judge me first
by the white hand holding my wife's
         purse?
An ignorant oreo'd ex jock – who,
         ostensibly,
forgot his African American based stock?
Am I forever to be a cubbyholed
         stereotyped tree
a democrat with cup in hand to comfort
         some
who would have my posterity rung
up in the stump that
avoiding open competition "brung"?

Love is in the Pit of it all
Love's Seed is that Pit of call
Heavily burdened – Our disobedience
    He does bear
even the smallness of our thoughts to
    His care
God's Love is the Pit of it all
Jesus – The Word of healing to enthrall
Love's Seed is the Pit of it all

Truth in Diversity

*"If all the children's minds aren't inspired to grow,
the posterity of future generations will never know
God's Purpose in His Plan for Diversity."*
Willie Naulls

The Christmas Holiday Season of my sophomore year found me, at the age of 19, boarding an airplane at the Los Angeles Airport, destination Lexington, Kentucky. Our team was a traveling group of about 12 players; Coach Wooden; one assistant; our trainer, Ducky Drake; and one manager. Our mission, as I found out later, was not only to win the University of Kentucky Invitational Holiday Basketball Tournament, but also to integrate Lexington and its hotel, movie theater and basketball pavilion.

The man in charge of the Kentucky Wildcats was the legendary Adolph Rupp. These are some firsts worth noting, because diversity is more than just a word of political passion. It is lives thrust into meaningful pursuits, cutting away at the core/root of separation's intent. All of us UCLA players believed that playing time was based on attitude, talent, preparation, and performance, without any limitation placed on race or other considerations. So listen to what follows to see and hear the fruit of Coach Wooden's team's **Truth in Diversity** planting in Lexington, Kentucky.

From the airport in Lexington, we were bussed together to the hotel downtown where we would be staying. What's the big deal? Well, Johnny Moore (another player covered with Black skin) and I sat at the front of the bus in Lexington, Kentucky, and in front of all our teammates. Coach and Ducky sat in the front seats on the other side of the bus. Johnny and I hadn't planned it that way, but the front seat simply had more leg room and we boarded the bus first. A first in the front row of a public or private bus occupied by African Americans and Anglo Americans in Lexington, Kentucky. No big deal nowadays; nevertheless, a first. The bus driver attempted an intimidating expression. We ignored him.

We all stayed together in the Lexington Hotel, A first in that town. Management would not let the Spirit of integration sleep in their rooms, so we were relegated to the basement's boiler room on little cots. I watched my teammates as they made jokes about the accommodations, but never complained. The humiliation was borne by each of us – Black and White together. We took turns showering and ate together in a special banquet room. A first in Lexington, Kentucky. I don't know where Coach and Ducky slept.

We went to their movie theater and sat together – A first in that little college town. A first. Coach was there beside us.

We played as an integrated team in their basket-ball arena which was, I believe, later renamed in honor of Coach Rupp. A first in Lexington, Kentucky. Coach was there to guide us.

The post-tournament awards banquet was integrated for the first time as I sat next to Frank Ramsey of Kentucky. He reminded me later when we were Celtics teammates what a fool I had made of myself that banquet night. In the midst of hunger lust, I threw a whole spoonful of horseradish down my throat on a piece of roast beef. He and a few of the local players laughed as I gasped for relief, screaming, "What in the world was that? You folks trying to kill me?" Frank said, in his very high pitched southern drawl, "Naw, Willie, I think you're doing a pretty good job of that yourself."

How did I feel? Well, Diversity in the making was a competitive readiness to play some ball, against somebody, anybody. People in Lexington were forced, for the first time, to see Black skinned people compete against White skinned people, and they knew that things would never be the same. I was eager to release the pent up rage within me, but within the rules of the game of basketball. Ironically, the UCLA team had come to integrate Lexington from Westwood, a suburb of Los Angeles, which at that time continued to deny African Americans access to hotel stays, apartment rentals and home ownership. In fact, such a restriction was in the covenants, conditions and restrictions (CC&Rs) of the home I purchased two blocks from UCLA in 1979!

Previously, I said that I had been called a nigger for the first time by an opposing coach before a baseball game when I was about 13 years old. Ironically, when the truth surfaced in my mind, I recalled that a few months before that incident, I had been referred to as that word by a little girl who couldn't have been any more than four years old. My friend and I were walking toward Dana Junior High School, up 15th Street in my home town of San Pedro when this child said, "Mommy, there goes a nigger." My friend shouted at the top of his voice at the little girl and her mother, "Shut up! What are you teaching your daughter anyway?" That was a profound question for my red-haired, blue-eyed friend to ask at any age, but especially for someone just into his teens. What rage hostile words about my skin color erupted in me.

In Lexington, where we were breaking barriers that none of us players were aware of until later, this big, slow, tree-trunk-legged player from, I believe, Duke University – in doing the correct thing by talking to his teammates aloud about defensive assignments, but in a voice loud enough to be heard several rows up in the stands – yelled, "I got this nigger over here." Now, my mother had taught me that a child of God should never lose self control over what someone else says. So as I positioned myself in a basketball forward's mentality, I looked into his eyes and perceived that his verbally demeaning declaration was a comfortable part of his vernacular. He appeared never to suspect that his words would evoke in me a rage to be taken out on him the next time I got my hands on the basketball – but within the rules of the game, of course.

For some reason, I had played very little at the same time as Johnny Moore and much less than usual that night. I came into the game during its latter stages when winning was up for the taking. It was one of those plays people make movies about. Facing the basket without the ball, I took four quick steps, in toward the baseline, faked, reversed quickly back to receive the pass from my teammate. Shooters, or rather offense-minded people as I was, love situations like this because the defensive player is most vulnerable in that he is lunging toward you in a desperate attempt to get back to where he should have been. This guy looked as though he were coming up in slow motion. His facial expression changed from false tenacity to horror as, with ball in hand, I faked to my left, and his knees locked in place. As I went past him, my left elbow of retribution shot out, plunging deep into the area where the jaw meets the neck. His head was hanging like a yo-yo from his body in lack of coordination as I arced the ball off the backboard and into the basket, putting us up by two points.

He came yelling down the court pointing to the referees, then pointing and coming toward me. The game was stopped because he was bleeding, and I was relieved, because Mother always instructed me to live at peace with everyone, as much as was in me. But we all know that if you turn the other cheek too far, you get it in the neck. So I was relieved that they called time-out to calm this young man down.

My imagination took over as I sat there on the bench. God was looking down from heaven, saying to me, "I allowed Coach Wooden to bring the son of one of my most obedient daughters from the worst poverty on earth to integrate satan's stronghold and you're trying to get Coach Wooden and all the rest of your teammates killed. Haven't you looked up in the stands and noticed that there's no one up there who looks like you? Willie, your dear mother taught you better than to respond to that word. satan uses some White skinned people to attempt to frighten Black skinned people into thinking they should stay in their place."

I sat there looking up at Coach as he glared into my eyes, searching for a hint of guilt. A referee walked by, looked at me and said something to Coach. I shrugged my shoulders as if I were innocent until proven guilty. In those days instant replay cameras were not used or I would have been ejected. But the whistle blew and Coach left me in the mix.

The game was still up for grabs and the two of us were still guarding each other. It is amazing how a well placed elbow, within the rules of the game, will expose a coward. This guy would not even look me in the eyes and stayed at a distance the rest of the game.

In retrospect, I think Coach Wooden had gained confidence in my self control that day in practice when a starting teammate intentionally sunk his elbow into my stomach. He had been threatened by the thought that I might replace him in the starting lineup and took his frustration and insecurity out on my stomach. Momentarily he took my breath away, but my response to his loss of control impressed Coach enough to grant me his starting position. I was rewarded for not retaliating in like kind as I did on that pathetic Duke warrior. Johnny Moore and I talked about those Duke University players later, on the way home. He had similar experiences as the object of racially insulting references.

When we arrived back in Los Angeles, my name was mentioned prominently for the first time since high school in the Los Angeles newspapers for the crucial points I had scored on that racist hoopster. Those points directly impacted the final victorious score. Diversity was on a positive and earned growth pattern through real combat and lived experiences. God knows we need His Spirit to inspire in young men and women that kind of competitive academic desire, to be at one's prepared best when one's performance best is needed.

Question: Can the spirit behind a well placed elbow impact diversity? Let us count the ways.

Within the rules of the game, institutional attitudes toward all its students have to be jolted into the reality of fair and just academic preparation for competitive standards. Let the most inspired and prepared students in equal learning environments emerge in fair academic competition against themselves, individually, alone. My contention is that if evil suspected that open parks with hoops galore would lead to our current environment of millionaire athletes of all colors, there would have been imposed a financial or other unfair requirement. Basketball, baseball and football would have limiting socioeconomic burdens of entry into those professions. Success in sports is our example of God's intervention into a segregated system to evolve into a free enterprise system, blessing the offspring of oppressed people with prosperity beyond imagination. Tennis and golf are examples of athletic institutions with limited access for the under-represented, but there are some Williamses and a Tiger in their camps. However, the under-educated, socially and economically disadvantaged will never compete successfully and consistently scholastically, because growth therein is information/knowledge/understanding intensive.

Inspired quality instruction produces inspired quality students. A good tree cannot produce bad fruit and, conversely, a bad tree cannot produce good fruit. Teachers are the sowers of the information seed and produce through their pupils either good or bad fruit. Teachers are the sowers of knowledge used on the road to making wise decisions. Committed, gifted, well trained teachers motivate students; and parents should desire these characteristics in educators. Godly called teachers –

revered, trained, protected and liberated to be whom God created them to be – will sow knowledge freely to our children in God's Spirit of Love. This is The Truth In Diversity which produces seed-producing fruit.

Many individuals in my life have, by overcoming great obstacles of evil imposed on them by others, endured their experiences to contribute to mankind. Let us begin with Coach Wooden. Why, you might ask, do I always use Coach as an example? I believe that God loves me so much that He put one of His brightest of lights in my path so I could eventually find my way back to His Way. He knew that I was prone to prefer the darkness and to pursue evil, even of greater danger than that which my mother had advised me against. So I'm so thankful every time I see Coach being interviewed on television or hear him speaking, repeating the same words he spoke to me when I was an impressionable young man. I thank God that Coach's words and lifestyle cultivated an already planted truth in me, encouraging me to pursue the course which prepared me to compete in the majority society, thus impacting Diversity. He encouraged me to look in the mirror and develop into the man God created me to be.

In the summer of 2002, my wife, Anne, and I decided to attend a new church's Bible study for the first time and, unbeknownst to us, the teacher's subject happened to be John Wooden's Pyramid of Success. The format was to invite each of us in attendance to put Scriptural meat on the bones of the words in each block which comprised Coach's success model. What does this have to do with increasing diversity? Well, the words of Coach's Pyramid, which describe a journey to success, don't include the liabilities of limited access. It's all up to the individual and within any individual's grasp. Only a decision away. For his words say,

"Success is peace of mind which is a direct result of self-satisfaction in knowing you did your best to become the best that you are capable of becoming."

There is hope for all of us in "them there words." Coach often quotes John Moriarty's words: "Doing your best, it seems to me, is not so far from victory." My parents placed me firmly on that straight and narrow road of "doing my best." I was blessed to have my parents' introductory teaching further explained through a medium in which I desired to excel and for which I had a passion. A unit in the diversity mix is blessed when he or she is exposed to a mentor who is faithful to do and live what "thus says the Lord." God's Standard becomes that brightest of teaching lights through the lives of men like Coach, inspiring his pupils to work to become the best they can be. Everyone can know that Light. Since God is not a "respecter of persons," He gives gifts to men and women as He desires, and through those gifts we have God's Diversity plan. When a teacher's will is subjugated to the will of our Father, God, "signs and wonders" manifest in his or her pursuits, and the fame that follows in and through the lives of his or her pupils is to the glory of God.

God is the Power to perform His Word in the life and circumstances of those who have chosen Him. He is Diversity's Seed planting for all youth. Ignorance is a disease whose cure is in the medicine sown by the Master Teacher. Can you imagine Coach Wooden's heart after he had delivered us back home out of Kentucky? Can't you just picture him, drawing away from the crowd of reporters, and further into his relationship with and at the feet of God? I imagine that he proclaimed, as did the spirit behind the mouth of David:

> My dear heavenly Father,
> you have delivered me, and my team of young
> men whom you have entrusted to my care,
> out of the hands of our enemies.

Although I failed miserably in response to the word *nigger* spoken against me by that player from Duke, I have long prayed to loose retribution's grip from around my soul and forgive all who have misused and abused me. The myth of *"The Man"* has never controlled my destiny. *I* have – in the freedom of choice given to me by God – and I have forgiven all who did not wish me well.

Lesson: "And when you stand praying, if you hold anything against anyone, forgive him, so that your Father in heaven may forgive you your sins." (Mark 11:25)

Watering Hole

College and university towns are like
    good watering holes,
places where students mature and retiring
    academic folk are planned for as they
    grow old.
Where 100,000 seats are filled in supply
    and demand's endeavor
while just on the other side of town the
    plight of Ignorance is all so clever
as to require educational preparation to
    get a job for growing
out of – and beyond – the looking to
    others for directional towing
toward upward mobility while smashing
    the fermenting caste system myth,
of looking at children's colors first by
    those who promote this miff
Ostensibly, busing was the step that
    affirmative action was to ensure,
the ceasing of the rhetoric – inspiring
    complaining parents to mature
for the opportunity was there for the
    Blacks to sit next to the Whites
to take advantage of the privilege that
    the closeness was to ignite
the zeal to know the secrets of
    acculturation's appeal
as if forced integration of the two spiritual
    poles would happen for real.

It seems to me that the shallowness of
those who made the rules
limited the depth of water for baptism
that participants could beneficially
use.
Beginning in kindergarten and before the
span between nine and ten
are the years of building of mental
muscles to compete in life – To Win.
Under-preparation during this time is a
malfunctioning potential
which releases yet another youth to
flounder without the essential
Competition's Watering Hole requires that
each child know about its existence
acquiring knowledge of its whereabouts
through parental persistence.
There is no better way to learn than being
taught by a gifted teacher
inspiring a child to want to learn to
become God's maturing creature.
Watering Holes are then the classrooms
where there's a quenching of thirst
where information sown in the proper
and consistent doses throws
Ignorance in reverse.
Jesus said long ago, Either you are
for – or – against the Love in Me
Learn what that means through
Knowledge of who I say you to be
lest ignorance, under-preparation and
poverty be your destiny.

As God's creatures can't survive unless
    they find His Watering Hole – to live
children suffer if they are not trained by
    teachers who will their lives to give
As the body without blood will die for
    sure
so a mind without knowledge will never
    cure
to mature according to God's Purpose
    indeed
Christ is sent to still satan's agenda
    against God's given Seed.
So – revere Knowledge, at God's Watering
    Hole, to grow
into the full measure of Him – in you He
    did bestow.

Levitating . . . .
Were There Racist Attitudes among the Coaches and Administrators during the 1950s?

Coach Elvin C. Drake, "Ducky" as all of the athletes called him, was Head Varsity Track Coach, Trainer to all of the UCLA men's teams, and most of all Psychologist to us, his "boys." He spent more than fifty years at UCLA, first as a student, then as the Varsity Track Coach for 35 years, through 1965. He continued as Head Trainer until 1974. Ducky was a man after my mom's own heart: quiet, helpful, dependable, accountable, efficient, hard-working, trustworthy, approachable, pleasant yet firm. He did his job without fanfare. He taped, treated and recommended therapy for rehabilitation from injuries for all the athletes at UCLA and we all loved him. His consistent gaze past our external characteristics into our hearts and souls to uncover how he could inspire us to work at becoming our best rekindled the fire in me at times when others in positions of influence thought I had only an exterior surface to influence. He, more than any of the coaches, spoke directly to me, challenging me, as he taped my ankles, to use my developing abilities and talent to the maximum.

"Willie, you ol' son of a buck, how you been?" His words, the twinkle at the corner of his eyes, the gentleness in his manner to his wife in public places gave us a role model of how to love and respect wives and women in general. He was a gentleman from the old school of spiritual

Elvin C. "Ducky" Drake

UCLA's Athletic Trainer

*Ducky was loved by all of us athletes
whom he called "his boys."*

foundations here in America. I surmised that his mother and my mother would have gotten along well in a world void of negative racial influences. I know, most assuredly, that Ducky wished me well. His positive influence on me was apparent when I quit UCLA Basketball during my sophomore year.

Ducky confronted me about my decision to exit the team after Coach Wooden decided to limit my playing time in games at UC Berkeley early in the season. Coach perceived that I would not compete to the maximum of my ability against Cal. His decision was directly influenced by newspaper articles before the game which stated that the Cal players liked me and had wanted me to attend UC Berkeley rather than UCLA. Their reported remarks convinced Coach to question my loyalty to the UCLA cause. We lost both games, 53-62 and 65-73. From my perspective he had publicly assassinated my character. I concluded that his irrational and spontaneous decision caused our team an unsettling emotional setback from which we never fully recovered. My teammates questioned me, "What did you do, stay out late?" Forced anorexia! He fed my bones to someone else. I growled and foamed at the mouth in silence.

Again from my perspective, against all odds – and in competition against all of what I perceived to be his favorite sons – I had earned a starting berth on his team. I lost respect for him because he made a subjective judgment based solely on what journalists in northern California had written in their newspapers – *in our enemy's territory*. I was livid. The glowing accounts of my reception from Cal's players were from interviews with those players, not me. It didn't make sense to me. I

Morrie Taft Scoring Two on Cal

Gabe Arrillaga of the Cal Bears, at right, became one of my closest friends and business associates after my retirement from professional basketball.

*Gabe and his family
– wife Kay and boys Randy, Jeff and Brady –
are a big part of my extended family of the heart.*

thought Coach had gone temporarily insane. It was like my senior year in high school baseball all over again. All of a sudden, a voice I had not heard for a while spoke forth: Could this man be a racist? I had earned a starting position and had never been so humiliated and disappointed in my life. I had allowed myself to relax and think that the color of my skin didn't make a difference to him. Now he had shown his color scheme and it was stark – bright – and damn near lily White. At the time my pride didn't allow me to think he would have treated one of those White boys as he had me, especially the one who took my place on the court, playing my time, eating MY bones. I was through! I experienced a new height in reality therapy during the next several days. I spoke to no one – except Ducky.

The day after our arrival back in Los Angeles, I went to the Men's Gym, cleared out my locker and said goodbye to Ducky on my way out. He understood but thought that I shouldn't make a hasty move. I told him that Coach had already made his quick judgment of my character. Coaches don't have to justify to players their decisions. I'm not questioning his absolute authority to play whomever he chose. What I did question was losing my starting position because of what he thought I was thinking.

I mumbled to myself, My own father didn't know what I was thinking. So how could this White man, who never invited me to his home or asked me anything about how I felt, deign to know what I was thinking? If he thought that little of my character, well, he could play those players with whom he was more comfortable – those who were readily accepted into Westwood housing. I couldn't find a permanent place to live and he didn't have enough respect for me to discuss a decision which dramatically impacted me and the community of Black people who held my success up as HOPE for equal opportunity for all Black skinned people.

My mother didn't raise me to not do my best and Coach had no grounds for what he did; just absolute authority to snuff out all my hard, consistent work to be the best I could be. What someone wrote about me in the paper was out of my control. He never gave me the benefit of his doubts. At that point I concluded that all of his philosophy written about a pyramid should have been veiled with an asterisk: For White Boys Only. "Peace of mind and self satisfaction" were hollow words with no integrity of meaning to me because they were from the heart of a man who, I surmised, had a double set of standards.

I went home to think about my options. I drove around Watts for a portion of the day and then really went home. The old community had not changed much, with young men everywhere idle and passing the time away in small clusters, sitting or slowly walking to an unplanned destination. Should I call up one of the other schools which were interested? I still had three years of eligibility left.

In the midst of these thoughts, our phone rang and my mother said it was Coach Wooden. She had a smile on her face because she had told me, "It's important to finish what you start. Be slow to speak, quick to listen, slow to get angry. Forgive those who misuse and abuse you, William. Let God be God in your life." Coach said in his earnest straightfor-wardness, "Willie, I made a mistake. I apologize. I would like for you to come back and play for our team." After a brief moment of silence, I said, "OK, Coach, I'll be at practice tomorrow." He hung up and my career at UCLA continued with a heightened awareness of its fragile nature. I had no power except in Coach's perception of my talent to win games. So what am I worth on the open market, I thought. When I hung up, my mind whirled around awakening as from a knockout punch hay-makered from my blind side. I would be more alert to the potential of all people to harm me. Who did wish me well?

I was very comfortable when I looked into the faces of my teammates the next day and anxiously awaited the first contact of competition. Every teammate was my enemy. I was all alone in silence, and I liked it that way. This encounter with Coach shifted my focus of character, cementing a bit in its axis of ME, MYSELF and I against the world. Although a poor excuse, it was still my reasoning for committing spiritual treason against the **Lessons** taught me by my mother. Mom, I screamed long ago, the system is flawed. White folks aren't fair. They protect the White boys and correct and reject me according to a different standard. The teachers and coaches are hypocrites!

From the selfishness of a benched player's ego: We lost both games to Cal up at Berkeley and our next conference game, in Los Angeles, to the University of Southern California. Our schedule had us playing the Trojans again the next night and Coach directed all of his pent up frustrations at me. I remembered at that moment that I had decided to stay the course at UCLA. Whatever he said were only words in his absolute authority. I thought he didn't care about me – only about winning games

Wooden's Threat Builds Sizzling Fire Under Huge Willie Naulls

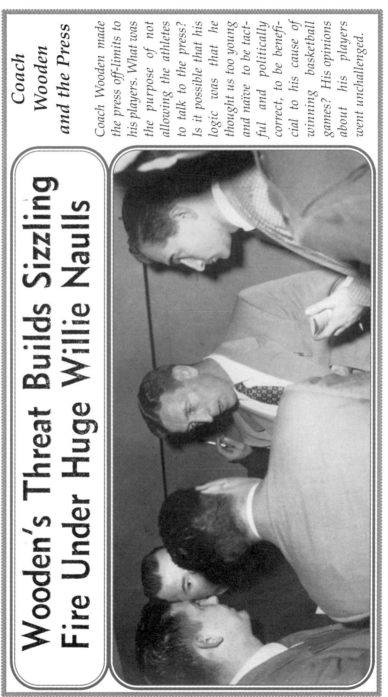

Coach Wooden and the Press

Coach Wooden made the press off-limits to his players. What was the purpose of not allowing the athletes to talk to the press? Is it possible that his logic was that he thought us too young and naïve to be tactful and politically correct, to be beneficial to his cause of winning basketball games? His opinions about his players went unchallenged.

using my talent as I passed through his system.

The headlines in a later *Los Angeles Times* article read "Wooden's Threat Builds Sizzling Fire Under Huge Willie Naulls." I remember Coach's remarks to the media after that game. He and the media had a field day at the expense of Willie, the Big Black Whale. And they gave Coach the credit for my performance in our winning effort. The sports writers didn't ask me why I had "scored only three points and collected only six rebounds in our previous three conference games." I would have told them that it's a long jump from the bench to the basket so they should ask Coach why he had given one of his boys my bones. The new voice who vied to orchestrate my decisions invited me to be quick to judge and speak, fueling my thoughts toward anger and closing my ears to God's instruction. That became my howl, to growl for more bones.

In the article written about the incident in question, the immediate implication was that I was an uninspired, lethargic, underproductive disappointment who was lazy, immature, not doing my best at all times, etc., etc., etc. If one did research on this type of article over any era in any integrated sport, I believe it would conclude that comments of this sort are made about African American players almost exclusively.

When Coach Wooden was quoted, try to understand for a moment that here was a White coach talking to a White newspaper reporter, whose job it was to report on sports teams who were reluctantly integrating athletic contests. These sports had an almost exclusively White fan base, and White officials who judged the rules and, of course, Whites who financially supported and profited from the

Wooden's Threat Builds Sizzling Fire Under Huge Willie Naulls

BY JACK GEYER

The dressing room was quiet as the coach stood by the door and glanced at his players before giving them their final instructions.

The coach, UCLA's basketballing John Wooden, wasn't happy. And he didn't keep it a secret. His Bruins, highly regarded during the early season, had received their third straight conference loss the previous night when cross-town rival SC had amassed a big early lead and gone on to win, 68-65.

. . . .

'This Is It'

Wooden fixed his eyes on a shy, soft-spoken Negro lad named Willie Naulls, a strapping 6-foot 5-inch, 222-pounder who made two of the tiny Bruin coach.

"Willie," the coach said, "This is it."

Willie stared back, wide-eyed.

"This is your last chance, Willie," Wooden continued. "I've been pretty easy on you all year because you started late and had a lot to catch up on. I've been waiting for you to come along and start showing something. So far, you haven't. You've let those other centers push you around, you haven't been shooting and you haven't been rebounding."

Willie's eyes widened even more.

Last Warning

"Tonight's your chance, Willie, your last chance," Wooden warned, "I'm going to start you. But the first time I see you getting shoved around or not scrapping, you're coming out of there. And you might not get back in the rest of the year."

Willie's reaction on the court was as though a time bomb had been placed in his hip-pocket, set to explode with the cessation of motion.

Since that night, Naulls has been a new man. And it is more than Willie grabbed rebound after rebound. He went after the ball the way a starving Great Dane goes for a pound of ground round. He shackled SC's rugged center, Roy Irvin. He battled and scrapped and fought. He scored 16 points in 15 minutes. His furious activity also cost him four fouls and he was taken from the game. But it was a delighted Wooden who patted his back as he reached the bench.

Willie returned briefly in the second half that night, only to foul out moments later, but the damage had already been done. His fiery first-half performance had pushed the Bruins to a 15-point halftime lead and they went on from there to win, 81-63, for their first conference triumph. A coincidence that the Bruins haven't lost a game since Jan. 16, the night Willie found himself.

In his first three conference games, two against California and one against SC, Naulls had scored a total of but three points. He'd gotten only six rebounds in three games, and a good player picks up that many by accident in one game.

Since then Willie's averaged 12 points and more than 10 rebounds a game, an improvement directly reflected in UCLA's present seven-game winning streak.

A late start wasn't Willie's only problem. Idle the previous season, Willie's weight zoomed to a blimplike 262 pounds. He now weighs a comparatively svelte 222, and he worked those 40 pounds off the hard way.

contests. They all had roles. Coach Wooden's role was CEO of basketball at UCLA – to evaluate, invite into, train for combat, control, use up and then dispose of all DOGS, including African American DOGS.

As I continue to stress, I was trained by my mom to respect authority and to do what was expected of me as long as it didn't violate who I was. Coaches had very few challenges with me within the context of sports. I always came to practice and games with the same attitude, to do my best. Coaches who practiced racism in any form should have taken Coach's advice to me: "Look in the mirror" before making character judgments about African American players.

In the winter of 2004, Barry LeBrock of Fox Sports News asked me a question about the above referenced incident reported in the *Los Angeles Times*. He concluded his question with, "Is Coach Wooden as good as advertised?" When he asked that question, with what I perceived to be a smirk on his face, I immediately remembered the situation and the embarrassment and hurt that I had felt all those many years ago. In response, I told him that later in our lives Coach admitted that he did not treat all players the same but each one differently, to try to inspire each to his own level of greatness. His statements to the press – that he was in my face, telling me that "this game was my last chance to prove that I belonged on the first team" – were made after I had had a productive game. The implication was that I needed his mental thrashing for maturation, to elicit my best effort. His remarks undermined my performance and enhanced his reputation. He had tongue-whipped me, his lazy and inconsistent sophomore, into a good performance.

A coach's job is to teach and inspire young men to become the very best of which they are capable. And Coach John Wooden did that for all of us former Bruin basketball playing dogs. His job was not to make me look like a fool in the press – that same press that he would not allow his players to face. To inspire me to be my best, I did not need, nor have I ever benefited from, violent and loud outbursts from anyone, but especially not a White male. That Seed had taken root years before I ever heard of Coach John Wooden. My mom planted that Seed of doing my best when I was her young and fertile soil.

I spoke often about Coach's two sets of standards with Johnny Moore, my teammate and an African American of high character. When Morrie Taft joined our team in mid-season, he was the third scholarshipped African American with under-developed but superior talent on Coach Wooden's 1953-54 Bruin Varsity Basketball Team. He would sit and learn as Coach used whomever he deemed deserving of playing time on his team (which he had the authority to do). It's like my dad said: "If you don't like what's going on in the house where I rule, there's the door." Coach's attitude was, If you don't like what's going on around here, I'll help you relocate someplace else. I had left once and now I was mentally sold on the long run at UCLA. He was only being himself – but so could I. When he decided that he wanted to give himself and the Bruins the best chance to win, I was confident that I would be playing the majority of minutes, getting my share of dem bones.

Stats are meaningless unless one tells the story behind them. Sports writers, even today, malign athletes by incorrectly using stats to measure a player's contribution. Wilt Chamberlain told me once that no matter what anyone said about him, he would continue to score every basket he could and grab every rebound he could until his legs gave way to retirement. He said, "Willie, that's the only thing people, especially sports writers and statisticians, will write about me long after I'm dead." He was right. Black skinned athletes are rarely glorified by their university or college coaches, sports writers or commentators after their playing days are over unless they are reluctantly referred to as the all-time record holders in statistics.

Coach Wooden's demonstrated lack of confidence in my ability to perform consistently produced predictable results: a Willie Naulls yo-yo season of up and down performances. Our team was an inconsistent bunch which never jelled. Maybe I should have played freshman ball that year, but hindsight is speculative and a waste of time at best. Two end-of-the-season consecutive losses to USC were the most disappointing of my career at UCLA. I'm sure a lot of Bruin fans thought Coach had made a big mistake with what some labeled his "give the Blacks a chance" movement.

USC was a team with exclusively White players and, according to the African American professionals who counseled me, their coach and alumni openly thought they were superior because of their skin color. They did not want me or any other person covered with Black skin at their school. Big Roy Irvin kicked our collective butts with his sweeping quick hook shots the first night and we

Two over my high school teammate,
Jack Lovrich, a Trojan now

lost the second night on a last second jump shot that ended our season. In today's system of 64 or 65 teams qualifying for the NCAA Tournament, we would have qualified and, I believe, could have gone far in the Tournament. But we lost two straight games at home – to USC! I couldn't believe it.

After all these years I can now better describe how I felt during the next several months. Anthony Hopkins' character, Dr. Hannibal Lechter, in the movie *Silence of the Lambs*, was encaged in three ways, including a steel mask and a straitjacket. His stare through the bars of his enclosure was riveting. Maybe my mental state wasn't quite that intense, but that image allows for insight into my head as I felt encaged in the expectations of my skin color environment of Westwood and the Dog Pound milieu of Coach Wooden. I did not want to talk to anyone because I thought that my play, even though I had scored twenty points in the first game, had let Coach and the team down. Especially, I reasoned, my family and my race – I had let them down. I was suffocating as I drifted further and further into self imposed silence as if in that cage. I reasoned that I had set integration into a backward avalanche. These championship games at home were not dress rehearsals. The season was over for us and I had to live the entire off-season listening to remarks from my hometown San Pedro folks and my inner city critics. "Willie," they offered, "that White boy whipped your butt like he was your daddy." Then the roar of laughter. In a rut between the White and Black skin worlds, I walked the tight rope. Nowhere to run – nowhere to hide. Harsh was the judgment – on every side!

I believed in my soul that I had let everybody

down. There were many faces which flashed on the screen of my mind: George Padovan, Sam Pittman Johnson, Coach Bell, Coach Martin, Coach Balin, Jay Wright, Donna Underwood, Sammy Lee, Herb and Lynn Johnson, Nelda Faye and Othal Lakey, Marion Helms, Miss Woodard, Iva Emerson, Earl Rayson, Stan Kobsef, "Goose" Gravett and his eight brothers and two sisters, Doris and Maurice Cigar, Vince Flamengo, Frank Iacono, Nick Trani, Mr. Ruff, Mr. Huff, Mr. Briggs and Mr. Lynch, etc., etc., etc. I knew that everyone of these hearts wished me well and I had let them down. Many others in our town fought the good fight of diversity through living together and allowing our differences and God given diverse talents to grow freely in open competition.

Most people in the worlds I integrated thought I was looking to be accepted into their group of Black or White skin. They were all wrong. I was looking for love to show its face to me. God is LOVE and I was looking for real LOVE from God through a person. My heart echoed the emotions of the blues song *Please Send Me Someone to Love* written by Percy Mayfield.

I was reminded, yet again, of a vital **Lesson**. Competition doesn't care what color the winner's skin is. It doesn't care about where you've come from and what your hang-ups are. I surely couldn't blame Coach Wooden. I thought that our team was better prepared than we had been all season. We just lost and I took it personally. For the first time in my life, when given the confidence of my coach, I had been outplayed by another player. Integration of the Races was making giant strides in the athletic arenas in Los Angeles, but nobody appeared free enough to discuss this issue.

I suspect that very few people will empathize with me as I discuss my selfish rage about the system of my youth that my mother raised me to forgive. She sang openly, oblivious to judgment from anyone who heard her, "Onward, Christian Soldiers, marching as to war, with the Cross of Jesus going on before." I knew and sang those words, but I forgot most of the time that she thought of me as a Christian Soldier, fighting a spiritual battle. She taught that I was in need of putting on the whole armor of God. Most of the time I didn't know what she was talking about, but she kept on preaching into me what God had to say about how to deal with racism and with coaches and teachers who didn't wish me well. She said, "God will fight your battles against people who are guided by agents from the very headquarters of evil. They are not fair and you can expect that you will be judged unfairly by them to hold to a higher standard, not an equal standard. You are a Christian Soldier so remember these Scriptures:

> *"Endure hardship . . . as a good soldier of Christ Jesus. No one serving as a soldier gets involved in civilian affairs – he wants to please his commanding officer. Similarly, if anyone competes as an athlete, he does not receive the victor's crown unless he competes according to the rules."* (II Timothy 2:3-5)

When I was rejected in baseball, I asked my mom, "Don't they understand that I have feelings just like they do?" I wanted to cry on her shoulder, but my mind wasn't free enough to allow that, not even with Mom.

She said, "No, William, they don't. That may be

hard for you to understand, but pray for those folk who intentionally deny you equal opportunities. Don't confront them. You can't win that battle, son. God is God and He will remove every force of evil who wants you eliminated for doing good. Remember, you are a Christian Soldier who has chosen to participate in athletics. You must establish your priorities to do it God's Way and not confront the world, as it is, by yourself. If you do it God's Way, you have won the victory already in anything you do which is according to His will."

My mental lenses adjusted in an attempt to understand what it meant to fight a spiritual battle. If we Christians are at war, and the enemy is invisible, working through people as agents for evil, what color is his jersey? That was too deep for me to understand so I continued to identify the enemy by the color of the opposition's jersey, in practice and games, in competitive situations. By my strength alone, I thought. But, by the grace of God, His mercy persevered upon me. His patient perseverance brought me to my knees before Him in thanksgiving and praise many years later.

Imagine how important my mom's **Lessons** were when Coach referred to me publicly as under-motivated to be and do my best. I knew he was wrong then, but most important to me at the time was that he didn't address publicly the issue of the race war I fought everywhere I went. I did not suffer from the mental condition of lack of motivation. When the plank of judgment was so prevalent in my soul's eye it was difficult for me to understand Coach's perspective. Now I know how fortunate I was to have been a part of God's plan to

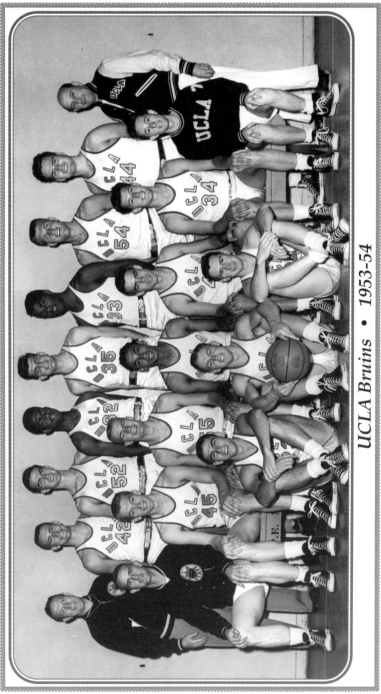

UCLA Bruins • 1953-54

Back Row: Coach John Wooden, Ron Bane, Don Bragg, Johnny Moore, Mike Hibler, Willie Naulls, Dick Ridgeway, Mark Costello, Trainer Ducky Drake

Middle Row: Assistant Coach Doug Sale, Denny Miller, Hank Steinman, Morrie Taft, Eddie White, Bob Ballard, Team Manager

Front Row: Lindy Kell, Ronny Livingston, Cortney Borreo

SOPHOMORE SEASON
1953-54 Bruin Dogs' Production Proficiency

25 Games: 18W – 7 L

Name	Season Points	Scoring Average	Season Rebounds	Rebounding Average	Production Proficiency	Season Rank
Don Bragg	280	11.20	185	7.40	13.00	1
Willie Naulls	212	8.48	197	7.88	12.12	2
Johnny Moore	277	11.08	141	5.64	11.18	3
Ron Livingston	313	12.52	57	2.28	8.51	4
Ron Bane	216	8.64	75	3.00	7.32	5
Morris Taft	141	5.64	67	2.68	5.50	6

integrate our country through college basketball. The coaching profession was led by the one man God had entrusted with this awesome task of being His co-pilot at the crest of the wave of integration, Coach Wooden.

Coach was probably disappointed that I didn't appear to make progress academically. I was finally hit with the Bombshell: Coach and I were in the same war, and it was bigger than either of us imagined at the time. He was leading me toward maturing to be the best I could develop into, mentally and physically. I admit, that revelation took time. Not being considered a class of people firmly settled on the back of my neck as an extra load to carry around with a smile of equal opportunity for all in my heart. What I learned under Coach's type of leadership was what it meant to "never do anything for people that they can do for themselves." When I turned that statement around and set myself in its path, I learned that I had to experience something before I could know the value of that experience. Sink or Achieve.

At the boiling point of pain in my soul, I couldn't have gotten any hotter. The evolving integrating foundation of collegiate and professional sports was not allowed to display the individual and varied personalities of its Black skinned athletes. Coaches are in absolute control over the life's expression and direction of their players. What an awesome responsibility and opportunity for coaches to do good.

Coach Wooden used whom he perceived each player to be as a potential role player on his team. He assembled his team to function toward one purpose, to win. Whatever he did for me or to me,

I now look back on with empathy, forgiving him for all the things he said and did which I perceived to be insensitive. I am in prayer that he has forgiven me for all the things I did during our relationship which did not represent the character model taught to me by my mother and often mirrored in his teachings to his players.

Voices

In the silence, of where I do hear
above the noises, where my thoughts are
    formed clear
come suggestions from two different
    voices
urgently appealing to counsel my choices

The decision is mine about which voice
    to trust
Even the unlearned knows information's
    a must
To make a choice that benefits my
    position
requires obeying the Voice that yields
    Godly fruition

Faith to choose a direction is a
    determination to walk
stepping out into the deep waters of
    which the voices talk
Now, there's this voice who cunningly
    imposes that wrong is right
But the One Voice who saved me says,
    "Stand . . . " in the good faith fight
The One Voice promises, "I'll never
    forsake you or leave you flat."
The other voice counters, "Did the One
    Voice who promised really say that?"
The other voice continues, "Worship me
    to become as the Most High's
    Choice."

The One Voice says, "My sheep who love
    Me know and respond to My Voice."
The direction of one's life is compassed in
    choices,
couched in heart's recesses, influenced by
    voices.
 So, be careful what you hear, and know
    that blessed is your choice
when you act in Faith, in the Good
    Shepherd's Voice!

The Night I Was Introduced to Bill Russell

The summer between my sophomore and junior years, my teammate Johnny Moore invited me to drive back with him to Gary, Indiana. His kindness took me by surprise and I decided to turn down work opportunities to experience a summer away from Los Angeles with his family.

As we motored north somewhere in the middle of Nevada, the open spaces were breathtaking. I kept reminding conservative Johnny that there was no speed limit in the state. He started calling me "California lead-foot." We both laughed out of control as I shared with him Coach's reaction to my speeding ticket, multiple parking tickets and book reimbursement scheme. He was shocked as he knew nothing about my first year at UCLA. I was impressed to know that the athletic department hadn't spread my bad news.

By the time we completed the 4,000 mile round trip back, Johnny's Chevrolet was sufficiently broken in. He was convinced we couldn't drive over 50 mph, as recommended by the auto mechanic who serviced his car before we left L.A. Our route was north from L.A., through to breathtaking beauty in Utah and Colorado then east across the Rocky Mountains and through to Gary – and back. The mechanic guaranteed Johnny, I believe jokingly, that his car would not overheat if he didn't exceed 50 mph. Every time he fell asleep, I eased on up to between 60 and 70 mph. A bump in the road or a swerve in a curve in the highway, Johnny woke up, looked around and said, "Whoa, lead foot, whoa!"

Johnny was a man of few words and impeccable character. His tenacious will in academics carried over into his desire to win in basketball. He relaxed and opened up at about the time we crossed the California border. Now we were driving in the open spaces of Nevada and, to my delight, I didn't want him to shut up. His stories about his family were special in that his life's experiences mirrored some of mine. We were the first of our families to attend a university and he thought he owed it to his parents to do his best. Talking with him in such a personal way caused me to evaluate my lack of academic commitment. By the time we arrived in Gary, just east of Chicago, he had inspired me to put forth more of an earnest effort to graduate on time. Of course intention is only as good as the work put into goals.

When we arrived at his home, Johnny's mom, dad and sister rushed to hug me with such enthusiasm I felt an instant closeness to them and a peace I had seldom known. Their home was in an exclusively African American neighborhood and Mr. Moore, who worked in the steel mills, took me around and showed me off to all of his friends and neighbors. I soon found out that Johnny's parents had the same Godly values my mom taught me. They told me they had wanted Johnny to go to Indiana University but had learned to respect Coach Wooden as an honorable man.

My time in Gary with the Moores was relaxing and peaceful. Mrs. Moore treated me like a second son. I had my own room with the privacy and freedom to come and go as I chose. She asked me questions about my family and shared her life

Coach Wooden
Johnny Moore • Don Bragg

These two team captains of 1955 had a profound and positive impact on my life. They were stable, dependable, trustworthy, conscientious, sensitive and empathic men who led and taught me to lead according to the John Wooden accepted and expected standard of leadership. I loved them dearly as brothers of the Bruin Pound and miss them both. They represented the ideal student athlete that Coach Wooden preached. A disturbing thought: Don is in the UCLA Athletic Hall of Fame. John, who performed statistically better, is NOT. That is a Dog Pound Shame for our Hall of Fame! It further proves that the institutional majority honors its own White skin color first, oftentimes at the excluding expense of Black skinned people.

growing up in the South. Mr. Moore and I had long talks as well. His eyes focused on mine the evening before we left for California and he grabbed both of my hands firmly. "Son," he said, "I'm real thankful to God that you are John's friend." I literally began to cry. Not one person had ever complimented me like that. Mr. Moore hugged me and whispered in my ear, "Yes, Lord. Thank you, Jesus, for Willie." Johnny was blessed with the father that I desperately longed for all my life. I always wished he lived in California so I could have seen him more often.

We sensed Coach Wooden's call to arms for his warriors was nearing and talked with optimism of the upcoming season. Elated to be back on campus, we eagerly anticipated combat and forgetting the previous year's disappointing season-ending losses to USC. Preseason practice began amid high campus optimism as our Bruin Football team was undefeated and would end their season as the NCAA Number One ranked football team in America.

Johnny and Donald Bragg were our co-captains. If I were to select players that I thought were Coach Wooden's all-time favorite basketball role models, they would be these two teammates. Both were conscientious, excellent student athletes and both were leaders on the court and in the classroom. By season's end, Johnny led our team in scoring and Don was second. I always suspected they were close to Coach's ideal examples of the men he envisioned his team developing into. Our 1954-55 team was his seventh UCLA team and we would be the most successful in his coaching career up to that time, with a 21-5 record.

The season began at home as we crushed a much

Johnny Moore and Don Bragg
Bruin Co-Captains
1954-55

from the back cover of the "Hoop" Program
21 December 1954

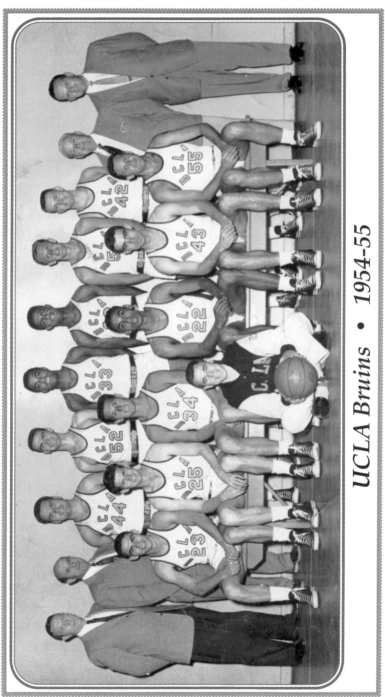

UCLA Bruins • 1954-55

Back Row: Coach John Wooden, Ducky Drake, Mark Costello, Don Bragg, Willie Naulls, John Moore, Allen Herring, Ron Bane, Dr. Ruth, Assistant Coach Bill Putnam

Middle Row: Lindy Kell, Dave Hall, Bob Ballard, Morrie Taft, Eddy White, Carroll Adams

Front Row: Manager

JUNIOR SEASON

1954-55 Bruin Dogs' Production Proficiency

26 Games: 21W – 5 L

Pacific Coast Conference Champions, Southern Division

Name	Season Points	Scoring Average	Season Rebounds	Rebounding Average	Production Proficiency	Season Rank
Willie Naulls	352	13.54	293	11.27	18.04	1
Johnny Moore	380	14.62	180	6.92	14.23	2
Morris Taft	328	12.62	115	4.42	10.73	3
Don Bragg	195	7.50	163	6.27	10.02	4
Ron Bane	275	10.58	104	4.00	9.29	5
Eddie White	177	6.81	64	2.46	5.86	6

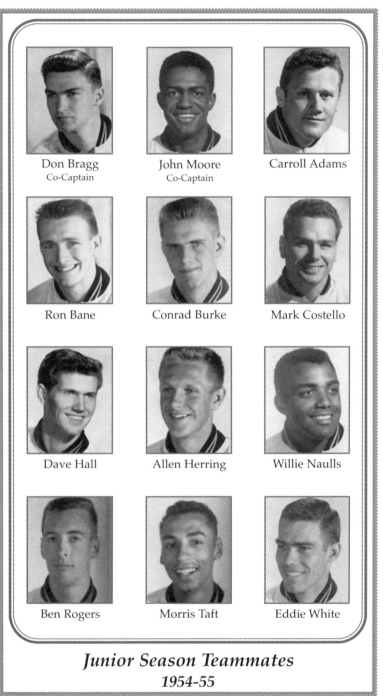

Don Bragg
Co-Captain

John Moore
Co-Captain

Carroll Adams

Ron Bane

Conrad Burke

Mark Costello

Dave Hall

Allen Herring

Willie Naulls

Ben Rogers

Morris Taft

Eddie White

Junior Season Teammates
1954-55

taller Kansas State team 86-57. Our next game was against the much heralded Kenny Sears-led Santa Clara Broncos. We won by 35 points and completely shut down their star.

Newspaper coverage did little to prepare us or Southern California sports fans for the man who would dominate basketball for the next fourteen years. As our team ascended the stairs of the Old Men's Gym, we heard our fans periodically scream as if watching Herculean feats. What we saw as we passed through the double doors was a wiry 6' 9" left-handed Black man doing "lay-ups" while warming up with the University of San Francisco Dons. The difference was that he stuffed the ball into the basket from a height and with more force than Angelenos had ever seen before. We were mesmerized and awaited with wild anticipation the next time Bill Russell would dunk his lay-up. We were not allowed to dunk and most players not only couldn't but, like our fans, had never seen anybody dunk like this. Bill Russell, smiling and confident, enjoyed the intimidation and attention.

The vein in the center of Coach Wooden's forehead almost burst when he finally arrived at court level and saw what was going on. He ordered us back down to the locker room. We sat like little children awaiting reprimand. He said, "We have come here tonight to play basketball, not to be spectators. Gracious sakes alive! God help us! Now get up there and warm up. Gracious sakes alive!" After a pregnant pause, accompanied by his equally pregnant scowl, he motioned us upstairs with his rolled-up program.

I shook hands with Russell before the tip-off and he said, "I'm gonna whip you, boy, real bad," with a smirk on his face. I stared back and snorted, "Can't you be more original?" He laughed and stroked his chin. We got the tip as I put an elbow in his chest and my hip in his stomach, and he staggered.

The game itself was a low scoring affair. Early in the contest I got my first taste of a *RussellBurger*. Confident after my antics during tip-off, I received a pass and faced him eye to eye. I faked him out of his shoes and cruised around him, expecting to momentarily hear applause in appreciation of my two-point basket. Instead I heard that deafening pre-game roar. I knew something was amiss as I watched the ball sail into the stands. A glaring Russell walked toward me with an in-your-face snarl. I thought, *This guy is uncivilized.* Was what he did fair, within the rules? The ball was going down into the basket and he jumped so high that his elbow could have batted my shot away. I glared back at him and couldn't wait to get my hands on the ball again. I put more emphasis on my fake this time and leapt with more determination toward the basket and – SHAZAM – he did it again – to the delight of our fans. S-W-A-T – but, with would become his career trademark, he kept the ball in play and, in the blink of an eye, his teammates were down the court for a fast break lay-up.

We beat him up physically the rest of the game as the referees let us play. UCLA won the game 47-40 – the University of San Francisco Dons' last defeat before going on a sixty-plus game winning streak through two NCAA Championship years.

Our return match was exactly one week later, on December 18, 1954. Russ was a madman who took his team's previous defeat personally. He single-handedly beat us. We deviated from our normal

All-American Bill Russell (#6) puts an obstacle in Morris Taft's (#22) way to a goal. The Dons' tight defense kept the Bruins lagging behind.

game because the Dons' defense anchored by Big Bad Bill forced us to look for him at all times. They won by twelve points and handed us our first defeat of the season. We quickly recovered and won the next two games at home against Colorado and New Mexico.

During Christmas, Coach took our team to New York to compete in the Holiday Festival at Madison Square Garden. We won our first game against Niagara 88-86, lost to LaSalle 77-85, and won the third place game by beating Dayton 104-92. The University of San Francisco, led again by Big Bill Russell, beat LaSalle to win the Festival's Championship game. New York was a-buzz with talk of Russell. He opened our eyes to what the future held for basketball through unleashed and free competition. He is the original force behind the blocked shot. Nobody had ever seen that skill exhibited within the rules of the game. Basketball was forever changed when the goal-tending rule was instituted to give all of us a chance against Russ.

Cultural New York City had an even greater impact on me than did Bill Russell. Coach took us to see Broadway plays, my first experience with live stage performances. We saw *Hello, Dolly* starring Carol Channing and *Pajama Game*. It was breathtaking. I stood and cheered and cheered and cheered.

The following week the bright lights of New York were still in our eyes, blinding us as we resumed our Conference Championship quest and lost our first game back on the road at Stanford. After that wake-up call, we won thirteen games in a row before losing two season-ending games to a team led by another man mountain, 7' 3 1/2" Swede

7' 3 1/2" Swede Halbrook was a formidable foe, who caught my elbow as I pivoted on his toe, which didn't impact enough the final score. The Oregon State Beavers ended our season in the NCAA Western Regionals.

Halbrook. That team eventually lost to Bill Russell's Dons, who went on to win the NCAA Championship.

The night I met Bill Russell for the first time convinced me that our beloved game of basketball could no longer continue unchanged. Through free competition, the game was reaching for heights far above the rim.

Basketball was forever changed by

Big Bad Bill Russell

Two-time All-American
Two-time NCAA Champion, USF Dons
Olympic Gold Medalist, 1956
NBA Player 13 years, Boston Celtics
Eleven-time NBA All-Star
Five-time NBA MVP
Eleven-time World Champion, Boston Celtics
Team Captain and Player Coach, Boston Celtics
First African American Coach in
integrated professional sports
NBA Hall of Fame

Big Bad Bill Russell

Big Bad Bill Russell
You'd best be ready for a tussle
whenever his NCAA team came to town
to defend his Champion's swaggering
      decree
I'm your nightmare's baddest Negro
who ever played this here game
Bring your lunch and be at your best
if you dare to want a piece of me

Natural corn rows hovering
over shaggy beard – he stared through to
      the soul
perusing for a weakness in the eyes of the
      enemy
he cast his spell of fear as he mined for
      NBA gold

Big "Russ" named Billy
swatted the best of PRO offenses silly –
      rebounding
for 13 seasons, striking gold eleven of
      those years
But even more impressive
was his boldness to wax aggressive
to stand in the gap against racial quotas
      and mystical fears
Introspective, aloof and private
to those outside his chosen climate
but to those whom he loved – a different
      view

Sharp and different sense of humor
especially when sensitivity was more than
    a rumor
They labeled him as one who over the
    cuckoo nest flew

Inspiring goodness to greatness
Through unrelenting and unselfish service
he made Hall of Famers – leading their
    talent to crest
Satch, Willie, K.C. and Sam
with Big Bad Bill, and as quick as
    Sha-zam –
giant stepped professional sports into
    competition's quest
to yearly express at its highest level
the Biggest and Baddest warriors ever
to compete against any and all foes to
    become history's best

The Lion of Basketball
is the retrospective foundation
of the NBA and the NCAA – March
    Madness sensation
He made college and pro championships
    his annual tradition
prompting both institutions to alter their
    rules, desiring Bad Bill's attrition

But, focus thought to note on "Russ" is
    his stand
to be a champion unique – and –
    respected first as a man
bearing fruit, as reward of his choice
in the character lived in response to
    Success's voice

He always gave his all
a full forty-eight minutes in his call –
    to play
each game – he wouldn't have it any
    other way!

I once heard our coach say,
There are two sets of rules on this team
so get used to that fact if you want to stay
One for my "60-Minute Man," Big Bad
    Russ, and the other
for the rest of you guys who are fortunate
    to with him play

I'll add in summation
that only through sports analysts' image
    inflation
can one attempt to justify a postulate's
    claim
that anyone before Big Bad Bill Russell,
and certainly none after who have
    entered the tussle,
can rival the impact that he made on
    sports' game

Truth's in the puddin'
and history will tell the tale
comparing the championship
    accomplishments
of my Friend – whom I've known so well

I LOVE YOU MAN ! !

Big Man on Campus

Returning in the fall of 1955, the beginning of my senior year, were Morrie Taft (our pre-season All-American), Carroll Adams, Conrad Burke, Allen Herring and Ben Rogers. New faces included Dick "Skeets" Banton, Bill Eblen, Jim Halsten, Art Hutchins and Nolan Johnson. Gone were the two men I respected most during my time in the Dog Pound of UCLA Basketball, co-captains Johnny Moore and Don Bragg. They passed leadership responsibility on to me. I was ready to be everything Coach's success model described. Were my teammates ready? I confronted them, old and new. We had formidable shoes to fill. Moore and Bragg were the best of all time in scoring and rebounding when they graduated. Ronnie Bane, Mark Costello and Eddie White also left, taking with them years of Varsity Dog maturity.

Practice was intense. Adams and Banton had a fierce battle for the second starting guard position with Taft. Herring and Burke came to practice early every day, worked hard and took themselves a position at our table of well-fed dogs. Morrie's early back injury delayed our progress until he returned.

Our first two games were in Provo, Utah, against Brigham Young University. The backdrop of the university town was the most beautiful I had ever seen and featured high, snow-covered mountains with a clear blue sky. I walked the streets of Provo with a teammate oblivious to the stares. The town folk were mostly blond and blue-eyed. They seemed unable to resist the urge to walk up to me

UCLA Bruins • 1955-56

Back Row: *Coach John Wooden, Bill Eblen, Nolan Johnson, Willie Naulls, Ben Rogers, Conrad Burke, Assistant Coach Bill Putnam*

Middle Row: *Trainer Ducky Drake, Allen Herring, Dick "Skeets" Banton, Manager Gary Walls, Morris Taft, Jim Halsten, Dr. Ruth*

Front Row: *Carroll Adams, Jim Harris, Art Hutchins, Jack Arnold*

SENIOR SEASON

1955-56 Bruin Dogs' Production Proficiency

28 Games: 22W – 6 L • Conference: 16W – 0 L
Pacific Coast Conference Champions • Ranked #8 Nationally

Name	Season Scoring Points	Average	Season Rebounding Rebounds	Production Average	Season Proficiency	Rank
Willie Naulls	661	23.61	410	14.64	26.44	1
Morris Taft *	324	20.25	80	5.00	15.13	2
Allen Herring *	172	10.75	143	8.94	14.32	3
Conrad Burke *	130	8.13	88	5.50	9.57	4
Dick Banton *	117	7.31	82	5.13	8.79	5
Jim Halsten *	75	4.69	45	2.81	5.15	6

* Only conference statistics available for 1955-56 season.

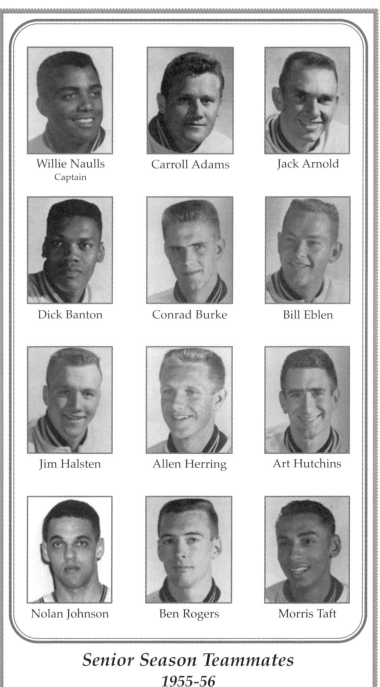

Willie Naulls
Captain

Carroll Adams

Jack Arnold

Dick Banton

Conrad Burke

Bill Eblen

Jim Halsten

Allen Herring

Art Hutchins

Nolan Johnson

Ben Rogers

Morris Taft

Senior Season Teammates
1955-56

This trend-setting move to outmaneuver the opposition and score demonstrates the theory that the mastery of fundamentals releases individual creativity.

Levitating for the Blue and Gold

Coach Wooden's Instructions:
"Willie, get them boards!"

and extend their hands of welcome. Lulled into a sense of brotherhood, we played like overly concerned gentlemen and BYU beat us in consecutive games, 58-75 and 65-67. We were already zero and two under my court leadership.

The next week's practice was more intense. We were determined but still searching for our groove. Morrie was healing and we were molding into a unit but still lacked maturity. Our next two home games were played at the Long Beach Arena against Denver and Purdue. Purdue's two All-American football players, Lamar Lundy and Len Dawson, were credible basketball players but we won by 16 points after beating Denver the night before by 28 points. Then we were on the road again.

We lost two games in a row to Nebraska and Wichita State, teams we would have beaten easily later in the season, before beating St. John University, 93-86, in the first round of the New York Christmas Holiday Festival at Madison Square Garden. The next night we won our semi-final game, 72-57, against Duquesne University and its two all-Americans, Sihugo Green and big Dick Ricketts. Although we lost the tournament championship game to the NCAA Champion University of San Francisco Dons, we knew as we arrived home in Los Angeles that, even with a record of four wins and five losses, we were ready for any and all comers.

Our team annihilated a much taller Idaho two nights in a row at home, then Washington State two nights in a row on the road the following week. We beat Arizona State by 20 points in our last game of January 1956. In the process I grabbed 28 rebounds, setting a school record for rebounds in a single game

*A hotly contested tip-in against the Bears of
UC Berkeley in a pivotal conference win.
Cal was favored with Washington to go
one-two in our conference, but UCLA won
16 straight games during an undefeated season.*

*With 39 points, this was my highest
scoring game at UCLA.*

which still stands. I watched my teammates mature and sensed their dependency on me for leadership. My heart was strengthened by Conrad Burke's improvement. Morrie nicknamed him "sixteen thumbs" during our early season practices, but Big Conrad was no joke any more. Allen Herring was the best six-foot-four-inch rebounder I played with or against while attending UCLA. Banton was a defensive tyrant, and he and Carroll fought for bones all season long. Morrie was reaching the potential predicted in pre-season publicity.

We eagerly anticipated our next game against the pre-season Pacific Coast Conference favorite Washington Huskies. Both of our teams were undefeated in the conference as we squared off at the Pan Pacific Auditorium. The game was close until the end. The score was tied at 59 with Washington on the free-throw line. There were four seconds remaining – no fractions of seconds on time clocks in those days. He made the first free throw, giving the Huskies a one point lead. Our fans moaned in unison as he aimed his second attempt. The ball hit the back of the rim and ricocheted high and directly out toward the foul line. I grabbed the ball at its zenith, knocking two Washington players in different directions. When I hit the floor, Morrie Taft was streaking down the left sideline. I shot him a bullet pass which he caught mid-stride 22 feet from the hoop in the left corner. He was in the air, levitating a bit before his release over the out-stretched hand of the Husky defender. The ball had a gentle arc, striking the rim slightly off a pure course. I tipped the ball in with my left hand as the final buzzer went off.

The Washington contingent protested that it was

impossible for us to have made that play in four seconds. But I celebrated, as shown above, with my teammates Nolan Johnson, Bill Eblen, Jim Halsten and Conrad Burke. We won the next night to distance ourselves from our then-closest rivals en route to a perfect 16-0 PCC season.

After our four-win, five-loss beginning, we roared to 22 wins and six losses at season's end, winning 18 of our last 19 games. We went on to become the first team in UCLA Basketball history to win a post-season NCAA Tournament game. The Athletic Department's Sports Information Office has attempted to downplay this first UCLA NCAA victory because of the subsequent change in tournament format. At the time, final season rankings were determined by regional tournaments. After our semi-final loss to the University of San Francisco, our victory in the consolation game earned us third place in the region, directly impacting our final national ranking at number

33-point effort in final game of All-American career

First UCLA NCAA Tournament Victory
1956

eight. My teammate and later surgeon, Dr. Nolan Earl Johnson, contributed 12 points in this historic game and his name is not listed in UCLA's historical records of Bruin players. This 1955-56 team and our fans are proud of that first-ever NCAA Tournament victory.

There is an inner peace when you know you have given your all. Every man on our team remembered where we had begun and the brotherhood of giving our all together. Coach Wooden had a way of leading: beginning with a jog, then a trot and finally an all-out sprint with purpose. Everyone on our team was the best he could be at season's end. I cried in silence when we lost to San Francisco yet again in that first round of the regionals, but our 24-point victory over Seattle University in that regional tournament, our final game together, capped the most fulfilling season of my career at UCLA.

Four years had passed so quickly, I thought, as I received honor after honor at the team banquet. Receiving the academic award was the biggest surprise of the evening. Studying had not been my priority, so I surmised that my desperate attempt to remove myself from academic probation between my junior and senior seasons produced a streak of good grades, launching me over everyone else considered for the award that year.

Finally it was over. Ducky Drake, sensing my insecurity about leaving the family structure of my previous four years, removed a large UCLA banner from the wall and gave it to me. "Nice career, you ol' son of a buck!" His twinkling eyes saluted me as a farewell – over and out of the UCLA Basketball Dog Pound.

UCLA Captain Willie • All-American 1956

First basketball player in UCLA history with a Career Double-Double

My Personal Best during the 1955-56 Season

Single Season Double-Doubles: 26

Single Season 20-Point Games: 20

UCLA Basketball: Top Scorer of all time

UCLA Basketball: Top Rebounder of all time

Pacific Coast Conference: First Team

Pacific Coast Conference: Top Scorer of all time

Pacific Coast Conference: Top Rebounder of all time

New York Christmas Festival: All-Tournament First Team

NCAA Western Regional: All-Tournament First Team

Named "Top Rival" of the NCAA Championship Team, San Francisco Dons

Consensus All-American: First Team

First player in UCLA Basketball history to average a Career Double-Double

Indecision's Cooing

What am I to do
now that I'm ceremoniously through
used up and finished
my value to all – diminished
no life-long goals established
I'm finished!
Mom's Voice:
Carry on from here
Stop and listen to God!
Let your head clear
Your fruit is what you've planted
      'til now
Change your sowing if you're
      disappointed somehow
You've been on your own four years
Nothing is accomplished through
      fears
Gather the weeds – bundle them to
      burn
Kick the dust off your heels, to
      righteousness turn

Situational Ethics in Basketball in the 1950s and 1960s

In the Crack

Have you ever thought about what it
    would be like
to be "In The Crack," Fallen, and taken
    for granted?
People assuming that you can handle
    "whatever's imposed on you"
by mean spirited people who cause you
    to finally scream, "Damn it!"?
What about that commentator whose
    hostility erupted into threats of
    violence
against the wife of an athlete whom he
    verbally attacked out of silence
as inferior to whomever the standard of
    his wretched insanity
out of his heart the cowardly approach,
    judging this woman's vanity.
Maybe threatened by Her Beauty, he was
    bold to proclaim
that she was a deceitful wife, an unfit
    mother, publicly trashing her name.
"A GOOD Name is to be more desired
    than great riches." (Proverbs 22:1)

What's your take? Is suspension for a
     time but a slap on his wrist
'cause a public attack on his wife would
     arouse a different twist?
If an African American writer, he would
     not only be banned for life
but all the Revolutionary institutions
     would embrace the player's white
     wife's strife.
Like the human rights groups and the
     against-child-abuse advocates of
     America,
why aren't they demonstrating in protest
     and outraged hysteria?
Violent words produce mental scars in
     children and negatively affect
     empathic folk;
but, above all, Duty calls for ALL MEN to
     protect their families against this kind
     of evil poke.
If A MAN allows his wife to be verbally
     abused by an out of control
     perpetrator,
whose punishment is "suspension" for
     ONLY a few days,
Should the message be to ALL WOMEN:
     Arm yourselves!
for the next wave of violence may be
     more severe in many ways?

Will young girls and boys who have
    fallen In The Crack understand
that it's up to them to speak out against
    any abuse and evil command
which disrespects any woman, counting
    all humans to be the same
uniting all of us In The Crack who Stand
    for Justice's Name.

Influencing behavioral standards by adjusting the rules of engagement to give a specific interest the advantage of guaranteed inclusion is unfair. It is generally easy to distinguish between Black and White people. If rules of engagement can be identified as adjusting to take away one group's inherent talent advantage over the other's, then situational ethics can be exposed as contrived evil embraced by those in charge of those rules of engagement.

If in fact coaches of the 1950s and '60s openly opposed dunking and influenced administrators to legislate against it because some players could dunk better than others, what was their logic? Dunking the basketball dramatically increased shooting percentages and gave an advantage to those players who could jump higher and were quicker off their feet. Why hold back competition seeking its highest level of expression? Many high school and college coaches thought that the fast break system of John Wooden sped up the game at the expense of perceived finesse and purity and

Courtesy of *The Los Angeles Examiner* • 9 March 1956

This cartoon could imply that Coach Twogood of the University of Southern California had the power of "white magic" to bespell jumping ability into the legs of his players on his all-White team.

ONLY GOD GIVES GIFTS TO WHOMEVER HE CHOOSES.

discriminated against slower, less talented players. Many coaches called dunking "showboating" and showing up the opposing players. In the school-yards of the ghetto we dunked routinely; but when we got back to our colleges, we were forbidden to dunk in practice and benched if we dunked in games. Coaches' restrictions retarded the expression of our God given talent.

Lesson: Unique talent, suppressed or reined in, atrophies in frustration. Succumbing to societal pressure to not allow the free expression of talent promotes a lowered standard of "competitive greatness."

Bill Russell was the first to dominate integrated basketball competition with God given talent. Lewis Alcindor (now Kareem Abdul-Jabbar) was the first to be openly punished by restricting his talent. College basketball institutions united nationally to outlaw his superior talent to dunk. Coach Wooden stated that in the long run of Kareem's career, eliminating dunking made him develop into a better all around player. The decision of those in charge was situationally assuaged and justified by one of its sage coaches and teachers. Coach's point is valuable because he represents God's optimism. "In all things God works for the good of those who love Him, who have been called according to His purpose" (Romans 8:28).

Both Mom and Coach inspired me to think. In my opinion, Kareem could have scored more points than any player in the history of college basketball had the rules not been changed to limit his talent's expression. He still would have won three National Championships for Coach and UCLA. As it turned out, it was Pete Maravich at

Louisiana State University who was allowed to express himself freely and now is glorified as the all-time top collegiate scorer with a total of 3,667 points over 83 games in three years, an average of 44.2 points per game. I remember Pete as an incredibly gifted basketball player who was coached by his father at LSU. The one characteristic that was popularized to describe Pete was "free spirit." What if Lewis Alcindor had been encouraged to be free, as Pete was by his father, his university and the national community of basketball fans? Instead, Lewis's advantage of superior height, quickness, dunking finesse was marginalized by the NCAA NO-DUNK rule. College basketball fans were denied his unique charismatic entertainment which could have propelled him to Pete's attained status of college basketball's most prolific scorer of all time. Influenced by the attention he drew to his university, the power brokers in the state renamed the LSU basketball facility the Pete Maravich Assembly Center. Had Lewis's talent been freed, would we now have a Lewis Alcindor or Kareem Abdul-Jabbar Pavilion with a Nell and John Wooden Court? Just thinking! Kareem most likely does not care so this may be a moot point.

The prevailing attitude at that time was committed to ensuring control over unique talent. If George Mikan had been as agile and could have dunked like Russell and Abdul-Jabbar, he would have been exalted for dominating the game. Marques Haynes was the first superstar of ball control and behind-the-back dribbling on display internationally with the Harlem Globetrotters. In college basketball circles, he was thought of as a clown with non-competitive skills.

African American players who attempted to imitate him to their advantage in high school, college or professional competition were scorned by coaches, players and the media as showboating clowns and were benched for showing up the opposing players. However, when Bob Cousy used behind-the-back dribbles and passes, he was glorified as the inventor of entertaining guard play, opening the door for the real talent to emerge: Frazier, Monroe, Robertson, Maravich, Hazzard, Dr. J, Magic, Bird, and so on.

The "purity" of basketball as was played in the segregated arenas of the 1940s and 1950s will never return because fans demand the show that open competition births. Segregated competition was counterfeit because it did not open competition to reveal true competitive greatness.

Sage Truth: Coach was asked by someone in attendance at one of his teaching seminars how he thought he would have fared in competition against Allen Iverson or Michael Jordan, since he is in the Hall of Fame as a player (guard) as well as a coach and has had his jersey retired for his All-American accomplishments. He graciously said, "Probably not very well." Most White Hall of Famers of the '50s and before did not play in the world of sports which I am privileged to have competitively integrated. One can't compare apples with oranges but can compare the environments in which they are grown and marketed. I believe that Coach Wooden, who was judged the best in his era, had he grown up in today's integrated world, would have been as effective as John Stockton or Jerry West. Competitive greatness is of the heart and has a way of rising to the top of its environment in any era.

My friend and pre-season All-American team-

Morris Taft

1955-56 Pre-Season All-American

*Quickness, speed, lift, suspension in space higher
than any other. Beautiful grace in launching the
ball, Morrie was superior to them all.
Great Track & Field talent.*

mate Morris Taft was as good a basketball playing guard as anyone in UCLA's Hall of Fame, including those who played on the NCAA Championship teams of the '60s and '70s. He and I were drafted by the professional Hawks. When we got to camp, he spent many evenings with White players who reported back to the owners and coaches, saying he drank out of control with them – and thought he was one of them. My words to him the third day of camp were, "Morrie, you don't have anyone here who wishes you well except me. This is war and you're treating it like a game. In this war, you are the best man, but if they get you in their game, you've lost already because their game is rigged." He didn't get it – but he soon got it – the boot. He was shipped home after the first two weeks or so of pre-season training camp. He was never offered another opportunity to play professionally to my knowledge. His story is one of hundreds of tragedies in the history of integrating sports.

A new Spirit is affecting self expression in sports today and has no color boundaries. Malone and Stockton, Bird vs. Johnson, West and Baylor vs. Russell and Havlicek, Dr. J's solo flights and Jordan and currently Nash, Stoudemire and Nowitzki have set a standard of high international professionalism. Reed, Bradley, DeBusschere and Frazier and Shaq, Kobe, Iverson, Barnett and Duncan are examples of earned competitive respectability.

Situational Ethics has taken a different and more rigid position in sports today. Both sides of controlled flamboyance have vaulted to the outer extreme. Synonymous with each individual's seeking the attention of sponsors is the potential of making millions of dollars. Players/entertainers are now encouraged by potential stardom at a very young age. They dream of being handsomely paid and showcased to fill sports arenas and owners' coffers for all concerned to divide.

My interest in the game has been spiked with the entertainers' show, especially so in professional basketball. I have matured to see the wisdom behind Coach Wooden's overall attitude against dunking and "fancy stuff." The game of basketball is increasingly moving away from its peach basket purpose. Competition for television ratings and fan loyalty demand that teams win and put on a good show in their fight to gain prime time exposure. Winning with style increases the winners' share of an ever increasing pie. The loyalty of fans, university officials and professional team owners to players has diminished proportionally as the competition for the winner's share of the purse has skyrocketed.

Winners of today's NBA and NCAA basketball championships mirror the schoolyard legends of inner city basketball lore of the 1950s and '60s. God is good. The outcasts are now being lured by advertisers, promoters and owners with multi-million dollar contracts. But – they have to put on a show that Magic, Kenny, Charles and Dr. J judge as the best of all time. It doesn't matter what I think or what any coach thinks. Not only must the show go on. It must put on a one-upmanship performance consistently or everyone, including Sir Charles, Kenny, Magic and the rest of Ernie's crew, is subject to being put out of a job as they all pass in procession for competition's review.

Words in Rhyme to Fit the Time

Just as an actor or musical entertainer
    was exposed
so a dunker or a behind-the-back passing
    star arose
With an attitude filled with confidence
    they did emerge
bolstered by fans, in the millions; to the
    box office they did surge
Critics cried hoodlums – saying ghetto
    image took sports to its brink
of losing choir boys' images and
    projected sport's reputation to sink
Consumers countered, Supplying the
    demand of the thirst in sports fans
    today
is far removed from where any sport was
    in the "lily white" day
Unchallenged finesse was honored
    through a separate and unequal
    media norm
until God broke in His Diversity plan of
    an open competition forum
Tennis and golf, and women's sports
    sought parity, contending for
    advertisers' bucks too
Without shame they yielded to
    promoters' tainted expressions in
    their "do anything for money" zoo
So Situational Ethics continues
    developing junkies seeking athletic
    fame

inspiring future generations to dream
	selfishly of the "exalting my name"
	Game.
What has emerged is an International
	ONE on ONE test
flaunting to Anyone, Anywhere – I know
	I'm The Best
Maybe Coach was right about that "in
	your face" thing
'cause it's promoting retaliations
	mounting for – "next time you better
	bring . . . ."
and on and on to quench the thirst of
	blood thirsty fans
guzzling for a bust, like in the arenas of
	Roman clans
where early Christian believers were
	sacrificially the prey
who in bondage were the antithesis of the
	combatants of "in your face" today
Less than one percent of college players
	make the professional jump
and those who do increase the validity of
	the game's purifying pump
proving that Race has little impact on
	what some did fear –
that White skin might be exposed as
	inferior –
but Larry Bird and Steve Nash have
	made very clear
that the world had nothing to fear!

Hall of Fame:
Is There Any Other Way for a Coach to Get There than by Winning?

Is "how you play the game" most important? Or is it camouflaged mind control of young athletes to serve their coaches' purpose?

Coaches are like instruments in war games. Some are sailboats, drifting, depending on weather. Some are aircraft carriers, prepared to aggressively attack the enemy at home, on distant land or at sea.

I am fortunate to have played for Coach John Wooden and Coach Red Auerbach, both aggressive strategists who launched attacks to keep the enemy gasping to refuel its combat units. The game of basketball is conducted to declare a winner. It does matter "how you play the game" but it's winning that matters most. An aircraft carrier is geared up to launch an attack, to win. Life and death are in the power of the equipment and how it is deployed. The driving purpose of my two most successful coaches who amassed victories in Hall of Fame numbers was to carry out organized, planned, aggressive and persistent assaults on the enemies' goal with increasing proficiency.

Coach Wooden had the bigger challenge as player turnover subjected him to compete annually against every coach's recruiting. Coach Auerbach's success began and ended with Bill Russell. Big Bad Bill Russell was the Aircraft Carrier par excellence, winning eleven NBA championships in thirteen years of combat, including his last two seasons, in which he took the reins from Red Auerbach and was both player and coach. Coach Wooden created and controlled his aircraft carrier system using many combinations of players over a span of many years.

Are there any coaches with lifetime LOSING RECORDS in the Hall of Fame? Is the Hall of Fame's measure influenced by player talent or what a coach accomplishes using the talent he has each year over the life of his career? "Of whom much is given much is required." It's not possible to accurately project what results another coach would accomplish given a specific coach's hand. Since Coach Wooden's retirement I have often speculated about what he would have accomplished with UCLA's talent since his last season of coaching. Bruin fans frequently comment on how differently a particular athlete would have developed under Coach Wooden.

Coaches encourage their athletes to think of the Team first, to sacrifice personal ambition for the benefit of the team. I concur with that philosophy – if the coach has the player's best interest at heart.

Both of my former coaches are in the Hall of Fame for one reason alone: winning. Not personality or moral or spiritual image. They won and won and won again, until their winning set championship records which are still unequaled. In today's athletic world, Hall of Fame caliber is winning. The two coaches orchestrated a new way to play basketball in the 1950s and '60s which forever changed the game: Press the opposition from the time they leave their locker room. Run them to the limit of their capacity . . . into the floor-boards.

I was raised on the charge that "It's not important who wins or loses, but how you play the game." A more realistic mantra would be "Just Win, Baby." Competitive sports, in the final analysis, is about winning. Individuals and institutions which lose consistently in professional and collegiate sports suffer financially. George Steinbrenner, owner of the New York Yankees, got it right. The rules in professional baseball are established to regulate how each team acquires players. They are applied and administered equally to each and every team. The only thing Yankee fans want to know is, "Are we competitive enough to win it all, George?" Mr. Steinbrenner's response has always reflected that he will do whatever is within his capacity to field the best athletes to give the Yankees the best chance to be World Champions.

"Just Win, Baby" is not of professional sports alone. Winning increases the demand for tickets and merchandise. Winning is highly correlated with high television ratings and making money, and money is the driving force in sports today. Coaches, athletic directors, general managers and players who don't win are fired everywhere at every level, as are CEOs whose companies don't experience projected annual growth.

Coach Wooden and Coach Auerbach are experiencing what very few coaches have experienced in their lifetimes. Their time and words regarding "How to Succeed" and "How did you do what you did?" are in great demand. Both are a few years from their centennial birthdays and are compensated more now than when their teams performed the feats for which they are acclaimed. The common denominator between these two legends is winning, not their personalities or personal morality. "Just Win, Baby" got them to the

Hall of Fame, not "how you play the game."

Final Word: If you are a college coach: (1) Get you some pedigreed DOGS. (2) Train and feed and house them well. (3) Observe all NCAA rules and regulations as you pursue and maintain them DOGS. (4) Above all – Just Win, Baby.

Imagination that Wins

It takes one laugh
with her not in the flow
at whatever she's attempted to do
to derisively stunt her will to grow
One laugh – joined in by others –
shocks the soul where imagination resides
Her mind suspended – a long time to
    recover
mired in the RUT where insecurity abides
Imagination is so fragile in flight
as to inhabit thought in the still of the
    night
where laughter directed is an echo next
    door
absorbed in the carpet which covers that
    floor
Silence of slumber calls the soul to alert
the resources stored in one's heart – to
    exert
whatever her spirit wills to share with
    another
in the uniqueness of him, a daydreaming
    brother

Is it the mind who relaxes
for one's soul to reap
what's deep within the abundance
that God gives one in sleep?
Or is it insecurities
caused by the opening bell's ringing
submitting your power to others
to judge one's talent in singing?
There's something real challenging
about standing up in front of folk
especially after experiencing
the ultimate brunt of their joke
Get up off the floor
and give it a try again
or you will miss the persistence
of exercising the power inside – to win!
Fear is thought a yellowing color
to be painted down every spine
which would turn and run
rather than in competition dine
Truth is – Free Imagination that Wins
embraces God's Power – and Faith in
       Him– twins

The Dog Pound Pedigree's Blood Is Thicker than Water

Eddie Sheldrake and Don Bragg, who shared in recruiting me to UCLA, contributed to the rich tradition of John Wooden basketball. That tradition's attitude spawns a real study in diversity. We came to his Pound's boot camp from a variety of socio-economic backgrounds and circumstances. We left the University filled with enough knowledge to succeed and grow toward fulfilling God's purpose for our lives. We learned that success in life was up to us, individually, and that infusion was in fact a mental transfusion. The God-sent opportunity to alter our thinking was presented to all of us. Coach Wooden continues His mission even today of teaching and sharing words of wisdom. Without Coach's input and inspiration in my life, I believe I would have had a different, more socially scripted journey.

I first met Don when he hosted me at UCLA's Spring Sing during one of my recruiting nights. Some years later I received a call at Madison Square Garden in New York City. Don told me that he was fulfilling his Armed Services commitment. He asked if he could fly up to see me at our Knicks home game and spend some time together. I was surprised at first but left a ticket for him at will-call. The demand of the game made me forget his presence until I saw him after, with a big smile befitting the welcomed reuniting of brothers. Again I was surprised that I was really happy to see him, and we left in the night from Madison Square

Garden to a Broadway restaurant owned by a friend of a teammate. We talked for hours and when the time was comfortable we departed, he to his USA fighter jet parked at a New York airport and I to a sterile Paramount Hotel room on 46th Street between Broadway and 8th Avenue in mid-Manhattan.

In hindsight, I wish I had been a better host with spacious living conditions to accommodate him for as long as he wanted to visit in Manhattan. The truth of the matter is I was still settling down in my third year in the Big Apple. I was less of a host to a former college teammate than his gesture of friendship to me evidenced. God has said that there is a Friend who sticks closer than a brother. That Friend in Scripture is Christ Jesus. He expressed His love to me through Don's deed of flying to New York.

After retiring from a ten-year professional sports career, I found myself again looking into the eyes of Eddie, that mighty mite of Bruin basketball lore. Yeah – that guy who, when I was being recruited, had me pushing his car up Central Avenue in Watts and whose smile reminded me of a donkey eating ice. Eddie appeared equally happy to renew and continue our relationship as Don had years before. My response to his question, "So what are you going to do with yourself now, Big Fella?" was, "I'm in a non-alcoholic night club partnership now. You got any suggestions?" He eagerly introduced me to Jim Collins, another UCLA friend of his – and subsequently mine – and I was in the fast food business as quickly as bureaucratically possible. This reuniting relationship fueled a desire to increase my knowledge about business facility and land ownership.

A developing zeal to succeed in business was a direct result of my UCLA Eddie-and-Don-and-Jim covenant connection. This continuing relationship with Eddie put me on the straight and narrow road to business development which is less traveled by most people, and certainly by most African Americans of the 1950s and '60s. It is necessary to enter in at the narrow gate called knowledge which leads to understanding and prosperity in business. Prosperity then is net consumable fruit produced in abundance. True Wisdom is from God and is shared through His chosen vessels. Wisdom is expressed best when those God blesses become His conduits to bless others. These men blessed me with no thought of getting anything in return. Prosperity from God overtook me and Eddie and Jim were God's conduits of love's expression to me.

A few years thereafter I contemplated buying a new home. After much research, I decided to look for an area where my kids could walk to the best public schools and educational environment in our town. I wanted a location where property values would continue to rise, where the community residents demanded encouragement to their children to develop their talents to reveal whom God had created them to be. My mom's attitude that revered God's standard for home ownership sprang up in me, and I knew I wanted to move my family to an area a few blocks from UCLA.

On the day I settled on a home that my real estate broker and evolving close friend, George Hicker, had shown me, I called a bank for a home loan. The person on the telephone recognized my name and said, "We have another former famous UCLA basketball player who is our boss and our bank's Regional Vice President." She put me through to this UCLA Ex, and it was Don, who had expressed the love of a Friend who is closer than a brother. Don, in his character, invited me into his world and gave me instant respectability with his Board of Directors and lending authorities. Of course their background check revealed that I had always paid all my bills and honored all my commitments, so they had much to work with. The fact remains that my friend Don was there to support my request at a very strategic point in my life's journey. Christ in him was expressed as the bridge over the lender's attitude gulf which a timely loan to me spanned.

Eddie and Jim I see on many occasions as they are still the type of "cheerful givers" whom the Lord loves (II Corinthians 9:7). Both of their lives have been a fulfillment of Scripture in that the Spirit of Generosity who influenced them to sow seeds into the lives of others has blessed them with multiplied return in their lives. They are prosperous, in fact very prosperous, and God is glorified as they continue to give, and give, and give to others out of their pure hearts.

Don went on to be with the Lord in heaven after his body failed him very suddenly a few years ago. I was told that he was fast asleep when his spirit and soul expired out of his body. Maybe he is handling some kingdom business; I don't know, but I do strongly suspect he is now in the presence of God. I thank Him for Don! And I lift up his family in prayer. Even after all this time, I still miss him. He always wished me well. His attitude was rare and is selfishly missed. Don was a man like me, tempted by the world's glamour as I am, so

I'm not glorifying him. I strongly believe that he did a Christian work in not judging others by what he saw. As do Eddie and Jim, he lifted God up and helped people who needed encouragement and a helping hand. So there are Eddie, Don and Jim – three blue-eyed BLOOD brothers in the Lord whom I love, because of the content of their character which allowed them to give generously of their resources and reputations to a friend.

A friend loves at all times,
and a brother is born for adversity.
Proverbs 17:17

Friend Indeed

Changing faces; switching places;
Who is a Friend Indeed? It's hard to agree
Revealed deceit from one's heart,
   displayed in actions – to impart
is what a Friend could evolve to be

Erosion in morality
causes increased neutrality
in measuring what one will
use for advantage;
a watered down plantage
revealing what the word Friend has
   diminshed into

Oh, to ponder, that way back yonder
God enfleshed Himself of His chosen nation
establishing The Standard of His unchanging
   measure
giving the world A Friend Indeed for its
   salvation

Because my years at UCLA, both as a student athlete and as a resource supporter, have been so integral to my family's development, I consider the people of the university as a whole a part of my extended family. Perhaps that is why I sense both a right and an obligation to offer my input. My involvement has been as varied and sincere as any other's.

There are many from my student athlete days at UCLA whom I remember with fondness and appreciation. Our assistant coaches, Coach Doug Sale and Coach Bill Putnam, were both gentlemen and committed to Coach Wooden. Coach Sale was very kind to me and Coach Putnam had the most beautiful wife we players had ever seen. Every time she appeared on the scene, players looked at Coach Putnam and at each other and said, "Coach, how did you do that?" Coach Wooden's system was so simple that, once exposed to it, everyone knew what everyone else was supposed to do. The repetition and familiarity of executing the system and its options created opportunities for each of us. So the assistants were willing and able, but seldom heard.

Attitude, talent, playing time and performance were the common components of all the players who succeeded statistically at UCLA under Coach Wooden. In later years, I heard from players that Coach Jerry Norman was influential in creatively introducing the zone press, a weapon we did not have to pressure opponents from end line to end line. I believe that we would have won national championships during my stint at UCLA had we pressured teams as did the later UCLA Championship teams, but that's only speculation which can never be proven. Those who live in the

Coach Wooden *with* **Assistant Coaches**
Doug Sale, *above left, in 1954*
Bill Putnam, *below right, in 1956*

past or future forfeit the benefit of growth that the present offers.

   Lesson: "Prepare yourself today, and tomorrow will take care of itself."

Life Is Not a Rehearsal

Life is not a rehearsal?
What is that trying to say?
Mom said, "Be prepared for each
      opportunity
that God will send your way."
Did she mean that there is no second
      chance
to succeed in yesterday's challenge set
      before me
if I failed to prepare for it in advance?
Hm-m-m-m-m

Life is not a rehearsal
could mean that every day
I'm required to be rehearsing
doing the Passions that God entrusts my
      way
Shouldn't I be conditioning my reflexes
so that my hand better coordinates with
      my eye
to perform what my mind gets my body
      into
from birth until my spirit and soul expire?

Summed up in my personal definition of
      success

is the demand of rehearsing at all times to
    at any time be at my best
while competing with myself alone
to withstand the onslaught of life's daily
    test
I should do it better tomorrow than I did
    it today
as yesterday's experience raises my voice
    to say
expressions bolder and louder putting the
    enemy under my heel
making every hand I'm dealt God's Royal
    Flush to reveal

Mrs. Gladys Savage, my assigned counselor at UCLA, commented that one's academic potential is estimated by the results of one's high school IOWA Test scores. I laughed and told her that my friends and I had decided that the test wouldn't affect our grades so we didn't even try to answer most of the questions. Of course, it was my responsibility to know entrance requirements – and parents should know. UCLA required a minimum 3.0 grade point average in core college prep classes for admission, and my GPA was about 3.4. When she asked what my high school counselor had advised, I told her Mrs. Suiter's suggestion that I concentrate on classes such as wood shop in order to prepare for that type of work.

Mrs. Savage never judged my previous counselors but encouraged me in my academic pursuits. She became a life-long friend and an encouraging voice to me and to my family. We continued our communication for years as she lived to the good

Dean Byron Atkinson

1952

*Dean Atkinson proved himself to be empathic
to me through the year I graduated in 1978
and beyond*

age of 92 years and went on to be with the Lord in the late 1990s. When I returned to UCLA in 1966, after retiring from professional basketball, to complete my degree, I enrolled in her husband's creative writing class. Professor Savage complimented me during that class and encouraged me to continue to write down my thoughts.

Dean Atkinson was another educator I respected very highly at UCLA. His empathic counsel over the years both forgave my unwise decisions as an undergraduate and allowed and even encouraged me to pursue excellence in post-graduate academic studies. "Mr. Naulls, it is my opinion that you have not begun to scratch the surface of your talent." When I finally graduated from UCLA in 1978, I thought of Dean Atkinson, Mrs. Savage and Coach John Wooden. I wrote and thanked each of them for their encouragement, patience and forgiving confidence in me demonstrated by their willingness to open yet another opportunity to work out of me . . . ME.

Don and Bonnie Sawyer became legendary personalities at UCLA over several eras of committed and loyal service to the University. Bonnie was crowned queen by those who wanted to purchase athletic season tickets. Why? Because she controlled, or at least strongly influenced, who could purchase football season tickets and where the seats were located. So the lady had much influence with those of us who wanted to better our season ticket location at the Rose Bowl. We all vied to sit on or near that 50-yard line about 30 rows up on the shady side of the stadium. Don did many jobs well during his years of giving of himself to the benefit of us Bruins. He was most famous for his deep velvet voice as the game day announcer for big time UCLA events.

Don and Bonnie introduced me to their good friend Captain James R. Terry. Mr. Terry was the police officer who wrote most of the parking tickets on my illegally parked car at UCLA. He was also the officer who reported me to Coach as a menacing nuisance who needed an attitude adjustment. Over thirty years later, he asked Don and Bonnie to formally introduce us at a Christmas celebration at their home. With a twinkle in his eye he said, "Willie Naulls, you were something back then. Every officer knew your car because you parked in the most unbelievable places – blocking fire entrances and in medical emergency spots, fire lanes, campus-equipment-only stalls and even pathways and sidewalks and grassy knolls. Made no difference to you, Willie. I was surprised to hear you're in the ministry now." We all had a fun time listening to the retired chief of UCLA Campus Police.

Captain Terry called me a couple of years later and asked me sincerely if I would officiate at his funeral when the time came. I asked him, "Why me?"

"God's got your attention enough to reform you from violating parking laws to the lofty position of being a minister of His. I'm impressed and I would be honored if you would commit to me now that you will preside over my funeral.

Anne and I bought a home in Gainesville, Florida, in 1998 and shuttled back and forth on ministry assignments between there and our home in Laguna Niguel, California, for five years. I was reminded of my commitment when Captain Terry's family called me in Florida. My heart sank in anticipation of facing his family, whom I had never met. My trepidation during the flight from Orlando to Los Angeles and drive up to Simi Valley was unnecessarily self imposed. I met Captain Terry's wonderful children, family and friends and we celebrated his life through personal testimonies and great stories about how he had positively impacted our lives. On my way home I was saddened that our families had not known each other. I resolved to delve deeper into the lives of the people God had put into our lives and not have funerals or memorial services reveal what I could have experienced during their lives.

Wilbur Johns, Athletic Director during my playing days, fielded most of the flack concerning my rebellious and devious behavior when I thought that UCLA owed me something. I greatly respected him for his position and presence. He was the basketball coach at UCLA before Coach Wooden and then became Athletic Director. When I returned to UCLA to complete my degree in the 1960s, J. D. Morgan had become the Athletic Director. Mr. Morgan's attitude was, "I'll lead; you will follow or get out of the way." His absolute rule of the Athletic Department and control over its policies of hiring, firing, paying and obeying were never questioned. He led UCLA as Tennis Coach and then as Athletic Director. J. D. Morgan took the national leadership position of all major NCAA universities to pursue, offer equal opportunities to, and welcome qualified African American student athletes.

Integration's fire was lit then and there at UCLA and began to boil over into the explosion of NCAA championships from the 1960s forward. In athletics

J. D. Morgan

UCLA's Best Athletic Director

we began to allow competition to be expressed in its best prepared form, and this produced increasing promotional and financial benefits for the entire university. In contrast, several groups in Los Angeles thought that competition for employment at UCLA was not to be seen as a subject to publicly scrutinize. The Athletic Department's purpose of winning games was pure and UCLA's overall expression was striving to eliminate special interests and racial preferences in most other areas.

A group of graduating UCLA students recently questioned me: Why hasn't there been a position-by-position analysis of UCLA's hiring practices since the '50s? Who gets hired and for what reason? Who suggests the names of potential employees and whose are the final signatures on the contract that hires each employee at UCLA? Is there an incentive to be just and unbiased? Do we have people in places of leadership who have a John Wooden attitude – to judge, train up and strategically utilize the best talent without first screening by the color of the applicant's skin? I didn't have an answer to those questions but offered the following: Unimpeded growth of an organization/university is characterized by open minded just leaders who are unimpressed by the color of skin covering. Talent, when judged solely on ability to accomplish a specific function, purpose and/or intent, opens up opportunities for all races. Coach John Wooden set in motion and led UCLA toward that Godly and optimum possibility.

How Did UCLA Attract a Black Skinned Baby Sitter from Philadelphia?

Philadelphia is approximately 90 miles south of New York City, down the New Jersey Turnpike which we frequently traveled via bus to play the Warriors (now 76ers) when I was a New York Knick. As our schedule allowed, I sometimes spent the night with the family of a player on the Warriors Basketball team, my good friend from Compton, California, Woody Sauldsberry. The baby sitter for the young son of Woody and his wife, Yvonne, was a high school basketball player named Walter Hazzard. I noticed in his eye a gleam of respect and genuine pleasure to meet me. I had not experienced that kind of earnest honor given to me before from young basketball people in the east. Later that night, I asked Woody, "Who is that kid?" He said, "He's the Philadelphia City Player of the Year. The boy is bad and he wanted to meet you. He wants to go to UCLA."

The next day prior to tip-off, as we prepared to go to war, I asked some of Woody's teammates whether this kid Hazzard could play. They replied that the young boy was the real deal. Out in the school yard during summer all-comers games, he'd loosen a teammate's teeth if he didn't have his hands up to receive a pass. He knew the game beyond his years and put on an unbelievable show with his ball control.

A couple of days later I called Coach Wooden and asked him if he had seen or heard of Walt Hazzard. He hadn't. Before the conversation ended I said, "Coach, UCLA is his #1 choice. If he doesn't make the team, I'll pay his way through school."

Walt Hazzard
(Mahdi Abdul-Rahman)
Three-year starting point guard • two-time All-American
Senior Co-Captain • NCAA Final Four MVP
Olympic Gold Medalist (1964) • ten-year NBA player
UCLA Head Coach (1985-1988)

UCLA's First NCAA National Championship Team
1964
Top: Ducky Drake, Jerry Norman, Steve Brucker, Fred Slaughter,
Doug McIntosh, Vaughn Hoffman, Keith Erickson, Kim Stewart,
Kenny Washington, John Wooden
Bottom: Dennis Mirrishian, Gail Goodrich, Jack Hirsch, Rich Levin,
Walt Hazzard, Kent Graham, Mike Huggins, Chuck Darrow

Coach said, "Based on your recommendation alone, Willie, I'll offer him a scholarship, and your guarantee isn't necessary."

When I called Walt and told him to send pertinent information to UCLA, attention Coach John Wooden, he appeared overjoyed and quite humbled that his dream was growing to fruition. He thanked me. His mom and dad (a bishop in his denomination) were thankful that I placed so much trust and confidence in their son and promised that he wouldn't let UCLA or me down.

Walt had a high school situation similar to the one I experienced. His academic performance there didn't qualify him to be readily admissible to UCLA, but he was allowed a different and better path than mine had been. During his freshman year he played in a local league on a team coached by my former UCLA teammate, Johnny Moore. Fortunately for him, he didn't sit out of basketball for an entire year as I had been forced to do by NCAA rules. He, more than any before, introduced and awakened Los Angeles to spectacular, exciting and effective guard play and leadership. Everyone he played with quickly got better, especially when his teammates realized all they had to do was get open and the ball would be there, in their hands, perfectly placed for grabbing and shooting. His passes were right on time.

When his sophomore year and first UCLA varsity season rolled around, he was ready to play ball. He continued to make progress all year in Coach Wooden's system and was educated about what Coach expected. The team experienced a disappointing loss in the early rounds of the NCAA Tournament. Walt and his teammates were excited and more experienced with each other as his junior year began.

I received a call from him one morning during the early stages of his junior season. He was thoroughly frustrated with Coach, who simply didn't understand "his game." After about 45 minutes of this collect call, I said, "What do you want to do? Do you want to go home? Do you want me to contact other schools? How can I help?" He asked me what I recommended. I remembered my frustration with Coach during my sophomore season. Trainer Ducky Drake was there to talk to, but I never for one moment forgot that Ducky was Coach's man, not on my side. So when Walt asked for my opinion, his plea penetrated my armor and reached into my soul. I empathized with this young Black student athlete who was 3000 miles from home and whom I had committed to UCLA.

"Let's review your options. First of all, you chose UCLA; they didn't choose you. The word that I have heard is that you have inspired a new thinking in Los Angeles about what entertaining, exciting and winning guard play is all about. You are a revolution who has taken the east coast style of basketball to the west coast. Coach Wooden has a system that he insists you play within. You'll have to learn to play within his system."

I told him that shortly before I was benched for the majority of two straight away games against UC Berkeley, writers glorified some no-look passes I made to teammates for easy buckets. Coach called time out and said to me with a scowl on his face, "No fancy stuff out there." I really didn't know what he was talking about. I had played guard in high school and could pass the ball with accuracy to ·

teammates with or without looking to "telegraph" a pass.

I asked Johnny Moore, a veteran African American teammate, what Coach was talking about as we went back on the court to resume the game. Johnny smiled and said, "Two hands on the ball will get you some playing time." Later that night we discussed further Coach's reprimand and Johnny said, "If you want to play, get the ball to your teammate like everybody else does. Don't do your no-lookers or you will be on the bench watching me play."

After sharing all these stories with Walt and after he had conferred with others, he gave Coach's system another try, but with a different attitude of yielding to authority. All-American captain Walt Hazzard had a productive career at UCLA, leading the Pound to our first NCAA Basketball Championship in 1964. Walter was indeed A DOG.

In the 1970s, Edgar Lacey, a surefire All-American, was discouraged enough to quit the UCLA Pound. I did briefly in the 1950s and Walt Hazzard almost did in the 1960s. Edgar made a critical decision about his future in response to being benched by Coach Wooden during UCLA's loss to the number one ranked team in the land, the University of Houston. In all cases, Coach was right. He made it very clear to all who would hear that he was the absolute, never to be challenged, ruler of his Dog Pound. If you didn't want to acquiesce to each rule and decision, he would help you find another place to exhibit your talent.

How Did UCLA Attract a Black Skinned Phenom from The Big Apple?

In the hallway outside the Knick players' dressing room in Madison Square Garden, I made my way hand-in-hand with my date through the crowd of reporters and others waiting for my teammates to disembark. I paused for cordial exchanges but kept moving toward the exit as we were on our way to get some food and then on to the Coconut Grove to see Tony Bennett. As I neared the exit a soft, pleasant young man's voice behind me said, "Hello, Mr. Naulls. My name is Lewis Alcindor."

I was startled due to the height of the voice's origin, and as I pivoted to look up into the face of this young man he smiled with confidence. "May I speak to you for a moment, Mr. Naulls?" he asked. "I am interested in going to UCLA and would appreciate your advice." About ten minutes later I rejoined my date and we were off to New York's famous night life.

Years later, when I was trying to impress someone that I knew him better than I actually did, I asked him to tell whoever would listen that I had a great impact on his decision to play at UCLA. The question "How did UCLA attract a Black phenom from the Big Apple?" can only be answered by Kareem. I suspect it was John Robert Wooden's philosophy, reputation and style of play alone that attracted him, but only Kareem knows. I always respected his parents whom I met in New York and commented to them that he reflected their gentle and kind spirit.

UCLA won and won and won – including three

Lewis Alcindor
(Kareem Abdul-Jabbar)

Three-year starting center

Three-time All American

*Three-time College
Player of the Year*

*Only three-time NCAA Final Four
Most Outstanding Player*

UCLA records:

First in Scoring Average (26.4)

Second in Rebounding Average (15.5)

*Most Points in a Season
(870 for 29.0 average)
Most Points in a game (61)*

Twenty-year NBA player

Six-time NBA MVP

Nineteen-time NBA All-Star

Six-time NBA World Champion

Naismith Basketball Hall of Fame

NCAA Silver Anniversary Award

UCLA's NCAA National Championship Team
1969

Top: Lynn Shackelford, Curtis Rowe, Steve Patterson, Lew Alcindor, Sidney Wicks, John Ecker, Bill Seibert. Middle: George Farmer, Bill Sweek, Ken Heitz, John Vallely, Terry Schofield. Bottom: Ducky Drake, Denny Crum, John Wooden, Gary Cunningham, Bob Marcucci

NCAA Championships – as a direct result of his decision and I had very little if anything to do with it. When I called Coach to share with him my conversation with Lewis, he and Jerry Norman were already in full trot to appeal to the Big Apple's phenom to come to the Hills of Westwood. We're happy he made the decision he did. I believe that wherever he chose to attend college with his scholarship excellence and superior Hall of Fame talent, that university would have been in NCAA Championship contention.

Two of my UCLA Dog Pound friends of distinction
Nobel Peace Prize recipient
Dr. Ralph Bunche and his wife Ruth

with the #1 Career Most Proficient Producing Dog
Lewis Alcindor (Kareem Abdul-Jabbar)
in front of Bunche Hall on the UCLA campus

photo by Thelner Hoover, UCLA '27

What Is the Value in Being a UCLA Legend?

Dog Ponder?

What thoughts has the one who doesn't
    return my call?
Is it punishment for daring to be
    discerning and all?
You know what I mean – constructive
    evaluation through my heart's eye
Am I now thought dangerous by those
    who conspire
to exploit and extract every drip from
    fame
at the expense of anyone who would feed
    their game
of only accepting one-side of truth which
    hides the pain
of the forgotten lives sacrificed for fame's
    inheritance's gain?
Just thinking. . . .

A former Athletic Director at UCLA, whom I will not name, made it obvious to anyone who would listen that he thought very little of me and intentionally advocated reducing my contribution to the foundational development of UCLA Basketball to an asterisked footnote. There are at least two incidents that come to mind which illustrate his overtly hostile attitude toward me.

A vendor from the southern part of our country

approached him for exclusive rights to develop a commercial poster idea using the names and images of ALL of the "UCLA Legends of Basketball." A Legend in Basketball is something that Hall of Fame committees have attempted to subjectively legislate as a popularity contest. Attempts to camouflage an earned status through manipulation of requirements for inclusion only further shame the university. This athletic director had to come to me reluctantly to get my permission to use my name and image because I had earned the distinction of being a John Wooden Dog Pound Legend.

I asked him, "What is the deal?"

He got sandpaper mouthed and laboriously blurted out that UCLA had a wonderful opportunity to get 50% of the net proceeds from a vendor's promotional idea and he thought it a great deal for the basketball program and athletic department to raise much needed funds.

I asked him, "Who determines the net?" Net deals are for college programs so desperately in need that a net deal from a vendor's speculation was all that was available. But UCLA Basketball Legends? Come now. We can do better. Especially with names like John Wooden, Kareem Abdul-Jabbar and Bill Walton. A net deal using the name of UCLA basketball legends is an oxymoron. My counselors in business while a student at UCLA had taught me that a nationally earned recognizable image and reputation should always negotiate from that strength and participate in the gross. UCLA Legends of Basketball should always demand a negotiated percentage of the gross, not of the net.

I sensed his mounting frustration about what I was asking him to consider. He blurted out that Bill

Walton and Kareem hadn't ask these questions, so what the hell was wrong with me.

I decided not to throw fuel on the fire he had lit and calmly told him that he should forget about using my name and image and use the more visible and recently established Legends, rationalizing that he probably didn't need my image if he had theirs. "If you can't intelligently discuss with me the money split of your deal with a vendor whose sole interest in UCLA is to exploit and make money for himself, and you don't know nor have control over his expenses which determine the net, I refuse to give you permission to use my name." I hung up and didn't think any more about it.

A few days later, the vendor called me with a disrespectful attitude mixed in with his Southern drawl and informed me that he had already printed approximately 20,000 18-by-24-inch four-color posters and that my image and name were included prominently on the poster – without my permission. "What am I supposed to do now, Willie?" he shouted, "eat these posters?"

I asked him calmly how he had gotten my personal home telephone number. He informed me that the UCLA athletic director had given it to him. I told him to never call my home again, adding that the athletic director apparently did not respect my privacy, contrary to UCLA stated doctrine. If he had further questions about his illegal use of my name and image he should direct any and all communications regarding this poster matter to my attorney. I gave him his Beverly Hills address and telephone number and hung up.

My telephone rang within an hour and it was the athletic director. Insecure men – especially those who have been promoted beyond their capacity to perform effectively – often attempt to use the tactical strategy of an offensive defense. I interrupted him mid-tirade and informed him he had exceeded my limit of insults from him and the UCLA Athletic Department under his leadership. I told him I perceived his attack to be hostile and personally threatening to my family's reputation in the communities in which we lived and served. In finality, I told him that any further communication on the issue of the Legends poster should be directed to my attorney. "UCLA Legends are, by definition, Hall of Fame filet mignon, not the dog meat of your 50%-of-the-net debauchery. UCLA deserves a negotiated percentage of the gross – not 50% of the net. Learn what that means and you will take a giant step in beginning to function to the benefit of UCLA."

In fairness to him, most undercurrent remarks about his lack of qualifications were from people who didn't think him qualified even as they influenced his hiring. The UCLA good-old-boy system promoted him based on seniority without doing a competitive job search for experience and wisdom. But he was promoted and UCLA limped and suffered a dramatic recession during his tenure. The weight of the fallout from the decisions he influenced during his reign are still negatively impacting the university. What gives me the right to judge? My voice is equal to any other voice of UCLA athletic heritage. UCLA's Athletic Department called me. I did not broach a deal with the department, but vice versa. They wanted to exploit my earned Legend reputation. Contrary to the distorted version promoted "off the record" by this man and his influence, I did not benefit personally from this poster promotion.

Another incident again reveals his overt attempts to negatively influence my reputation at UCLA. One of the honors I received as an entrepreneur and philanthropist after completing careers at UCLA and in professional basketball was the prestigious NCAA Silver Anniversary Award. It is given to honor selected All-American basketball players judged to have contributed the most to our society during the 25 years following their last season of university competition. The above referenced Athletic Director and his Athletic Department intentionally omitted my name from the list of the three UCLA athletes so honored. Kareem Abdul-Jabbar and Bill Walton were featured in Bruin athletic publications as being the only two so honored. I was the first former UCLA basketball player honored by the NCAA with this award and the first, I believe, ever to be intentionally omitted from his or her university's publications.

His department, I'm told, deleted my files in the Sports Information Department, removing most of the photos and accumulated history of my performance as a basketball player at UCLA. That's mean spirited at best. The real question is how deep was his pollution. Who else was on his hit list? My family and friends were shocked by his boldness of assumed authority. Black alumni are reviewing his regime's work of distorting the accomplishments of some and promoting the mediocrity of others.

This former athletic director doesn't like me and I must admit that I don't respect him. I comment on behalf of all the Black UCLA athletes who have been insensitively abused by people like

Daily
Bruin

"Bowl
Issue"

12/11/00

Star player of '50s helped lay foundation for UCLA greatness

FEATURE: William Naulls followed a stellar Bruin career with 5 NBA titles

By AJ Cadman
Daily Bruin Senior Staff

With the 11 national championships, 52 consecutive winning seasons and 27 conference championships, it's easy to reminisce about the glory of the UCLA men's basketball program.

But with the success, it's easy to forget those who laid the bricks of Bruin basketball.

Sure, Lew Alcindor and Bill Walton are Hall of Fame centers who helped lead UCLA to five national titles in the late 1960s and early 1970s.

But only one other Bruin has averaged a double-double during his career in the blue and gold – William Naulls. He nearly did the same in a 10-year NBA career with four teams, during which he helped the Boston Celtics to three of their record 16 titles, from 1963 to 1966.

On March 16, 1956, Daily Bruin basketball beat writer Chuck Fenton wrote, "Of course replacing Naulls is like asking for a miracle. It has taken Wooden 20 years in the game of basketball to come up with a Naulls, who he called, 'the greatest player I ever coached.'"

Naulls was the first in a long line of

Naulls wasn't exactly the prototypical big man.

Playing back in the era where freshmen were forced to sit out their first season, "the Whale" posted averages of 15.5 points and 11.4 rebounds per game over his three-year UCLA career.

In 1956, when professional basketball grabbed headlines on the Eastern seaboard, Naulls was transforming West Coast basketball.

It was a senior season that saw him drop 23.6 points and grab 14.6 boards every night he took the floor. He helped the Bruins garner a 22-6 overall record and the first of eight perfect conference records (16-0) Pacific Coast Conference) under Wooden.

> "It has taken Wooden 20 years ... to come up with a Naulls.
>
> **Chuck Fenton**
> 1956 Daily Bruin sports writer

Naulls, not exactly one the largest players in school history, scored a personal-best 39 points on March 2 of that season against California. Naulls held the UCLA record until Gail

Hall of Famer Pete Newell, remarked after that game, referring to the Bruin center's runner-up position behind 6-foot-10 San Francisco shotblocker Bill Russell.

But perhaps his crowning UCLA achievement was set earlier that year on Jan. 28. Naulls pulled down 28 rebounds in a 99-79 blowout of Arizona State – a record that still stands in the Bruin record books.

That year in the NCAA first round, UCLA would face Russell and USF, giving the undersized Naulls an opportunity to go eye-to-eye with the nation's top player.

USF went on to win the national title that year, but the match-up was repeated a year later during both centers' senior seasons.

Russell scored 21 against UCLA in a 72-61 victory in Corvallis, Ore. Naulls managed to lead the Bruins with 16 points to claim the school's career scoring record, but Russell went on to win his second consecutive NCAA men's basketball title.

Naulls earned first team-All-Pacific Coast Conference and All-America honors for his amazing senior season in 1956. Then, the National Basketball Association came calling.

What Russell saw from Naulls throughout their college showdowns would resurface seven years later when he urged Celtic head coach Red Auerbach to acquire Naulls.

A second-round draft pick by the

UCLA Sports Information

William Naulls, No. 33, is one of only three Bruins ever to average a double-double throughout his career as a player at UCLA.

him. Great athletic tradition is built on the solid foundation of truth in accurately reporting individual and team accomplishments. When that process is polluted by men who selfishly want history to reflect their myopic and oftentimes racist views, the integrity of the university is undermined.

My family has invested our human and financial resources in the fertile soil at UCLA. I was the first former Bruin Basketball player – and one of only three, the others being Pooh Richardson and Carroll Adams – to endow a basketball scholarship at UCLA. We are here for the long run and our watering is to assure that UCLA produces a diverse and good harvest.

Some will cry *foul* that an accepted member of its inner circle would speak forth truths publicly. Who better than I who has experienced for more years than most (except Coach Wooden and a few others) the complacency of status quo here in Bruinville even as other universities across the country – even in the deepest of our Southern states – have swept by us in the arena of cultural and racial sensitivity, especially in employment opportunities.

> Black Folk and White Folk
> like rhythm and blues
> historically wed partners
> now paying some dues . . . .

Give 'em Heaven

If what's growing up around you reeks of
    rot
indicating leaven planting of a satanic
    plot
could be that there's an implosion of the
    good intended seeds
choking from inattentive watering and the
    invading weeds.

First collect the weeds and bundle them
    to be burned
then gather the wheat as God's Word
    returned.
Draw near to God in a humble state of
    submission
and He will lift your crop up as His
    promised fruition.

For God puts His "good pleasure
    increase" into every seed He gives
to demonstrate His faithfulness, that the
    world might know Christ lives!
So, when you detect signs of satanic
    leaven
submit to God, resist the devil, and
    Give 'em Heaven!

Pedigree Reunion at the Bruin Dog Pound
for a Good Cause

In 1974 I became the Chairman of the UCLA Alumni Association's Ralph Bunche Scholarship Committee. Money and interest in minority scholarships were at a low ebb and previous fundraisers had not been successful. In order to provide much needed funds I proposed that we enlist members of the Bruin Dog Pound Pedigree to come together again in a benefit basketball game against a group of selected NBA players. The Association entrusted me with the responsibility of procuring the players, advertising and promoting the event, and contracting for all goods and services from on- and off-campus vendors. I insisted on having exclusive accountability for everything associated with the event, including all revenue and expenses. Don Bragg, my former teammate and then Regional Vice President of Great Western Savings, and I controlled all of the finances through a joint account I set up at his institution.

The game was staged at UCLA's Pauley Pavilion before a sell-out crowd of Hollywood stars and enthusiastic fans of UCLA's rich NCAA Championship heritage. I coached a team of NBA stars who had been among the most proficient and productive of all former Bruin Dogs. Jerry West coached the opposing team consisting of NBA All-Stars who had attended other colleges and universities. All of these athletes united to give of their name and fame to raise money for scholarships for deserving disadvantaged American-born

Three All-American Pedigreed Bruin Dogs and their Wise Counselor

Curtis Rowe · CMPP # *6*

Walt Hazzard (Mahdi Abdul-Rahman) · CMPP # *23*

Dr. Winston Doby
then Vice Chancellor, Student Affairs
currently University of California Vice President

Sidney Wicks · CMPP # *5*

gathering at the BBQ prior to the basketball game between former UCLA Bruin Dogs and NBA All-Stars organized by Willie Naulls to benefit the Ralph Bunche Scholarship Fund at UCLA

1974

UCLA Alumni Association President
Jim Collins
introducing
Mrs. Ruth Bunche

Ralph Bunche Scholarship Fund
Charity Basketball Game

Pauley Pavilion, UCLA
1974

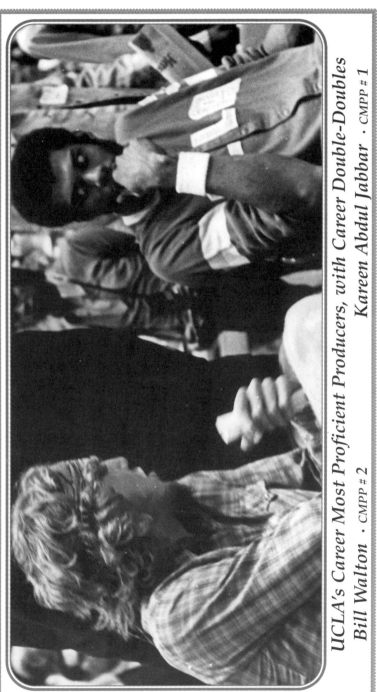

UCLA's Career Most Proficient Producers, with Career Double-Doubles
Kareen Abdul Jabbar · CMPP # 1
Bill Walton · CMPP # 2

UCLA's Career Most Proficient Producers, with Career Double-Doubles

Bill Walton · CMPP # 2   *Willie Naulls* · CMPP # 3

UCLA's Career Most Proficient Producers give back in the Bunche Charity Game
Bill Walton #2 • Gail Goodrich #16 • Walt Hazzard #23 • "Coach" Willie #3 • Curtis Rowe #6

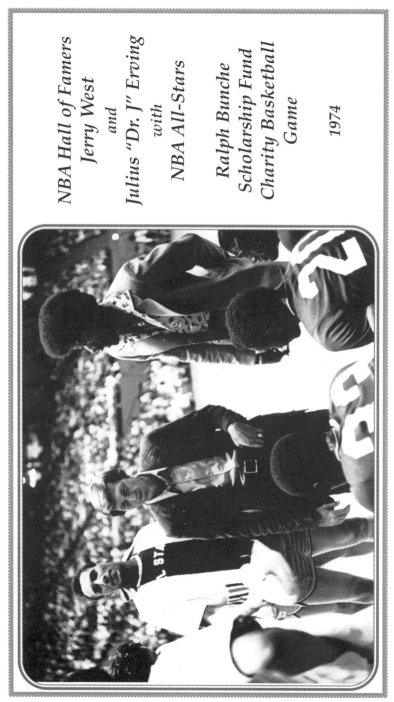

NBA Hall of Famers
Jerry West
and
Julius "Dr. J" Erving
with
NBA All-Stars

Ralph Bunche
Scholarship Fund
Charity Basketball
Game

1974

Hall of Famers Ducky Drake and Bill Walton with Dr. Augustus A. White

Lisa Naulls   Jacke Horne   Mrs. Ruth Bunche   Elsner Horne

Augustus A. White, III, M.D., Ph.D.

Professor, Harvard Medical School
Orthopaedic Surgeon-In-Chief, Beth Israel Deaconess
Medical Center

came from Boston to volunteer as the
official physician to the athletes

minority students. The event was the most successful of any fundraiser of its kind in the history of UCLA Athletics. We not only netted more money (approximately $100,000), but reunited Bruin Dog Pound Pedigrees with peers, fans, coaches and administrators.

UCLA Athletic Hall of Fame: Who Gets There? How and When?

The UCLA Athletic Hall of Fame was established in 1984 to honor those who had excelled in competing for the Blue and Gold. Choosing players to be honored has been an inexact science at best. Although I am convinced it was well intended, the process is subjective. The foundational doctrine of the charter membership of legend makers selected by the athletic director, his department and administration representatives instituted a system of subjective voting power influenced heavily by whether the committee members had seen a particular nominee perform or had preferences based upon an athlete's reputation. I contend that the system was devised to establish control over the possibility of an objective evaluation of individual players' career production proficiency. In many cases those individuals selected, all deserving of recognition, are promoted by special interests and emotional appeals that don't honor the weight of an objective, well thought out approach to a statistical analysis of competitive career performance. Determining the effectiveness of individual athletes during their times of glory in a given sport should be the goal.

I am convinced that everyone in the Hall of

Fame belongs there because of the athletes' individual contributions and accomplishments. Most important to me and many others of like persuasion is whether the athletic department, by following its doctrine in its unchallenged way, has served all of its former athletes fairly. Hindsight is always potentially critical but, in the world of progress and growth, constructive analysis is better labeled "debriefing" in order that things are done better from any given point forward. Would it not have been more efficient to evaluate players by era when considering Hall of Fame inductees for inclusion? How can an athlete from the 1940s be a Hall of Fame inductee in 2005 and not have been a Hall of Famer of the charter group, or soon thereafter? He or she then becomes a Hall of Famer who was subjectively excluded by the power of popular votes until being nominated and chosen subjectively by the athletic director, his chosen and invited committee and his entourage of ex-officios.

My 1950s teammate Johnny Moore comes to mind. He has not been proposed, advocated for or voted into the Hall of Fame. Our teammate Don Bragg is a 1994 inductee. Johnny and Don were co-captains of our teams. One graduated as the all-time scorer, the other as the all-time rebounder in UCLA history. Both were outstanding student athletes and Coach Wooden's favorite examples of role models for his program. Johnny and Don were both All-Americans. Both lived exemplary lives as family men in the financial corporate world of their choosing. Don Bragg is in the Hall of Fame. Johnny Moore is not. Eddie Sheldrake, Fred Slaughter, Kenny Washington and Keith Erickson, while not All-Americans, are in the Hall of Fame.

All-American Walt Torrence is not. What about the case of All-American Rommie Loudd who played both ways for football glory? His teammate Hardiman Cureton is finally being inducted this year, my first on the Hall of Fame committee. In the vernacular of our Bruin Pound, it's a UCLA Dog Pound Shame that Loudd is not included. My point here is that the athletic department's method and doctrine of selecting Hall of Fame members is subjective and excludes objective performance comparisons. It should make Coach Wooden very uncomfortable when he observes the unfolding drama created by the myopic decisions made by our athletic department when establishing the UCLA Athletic Hall of Fame.

I reiterate, every person in the Hall of Fame deserves to be there. My intent is not to dishonor those men and women and their families. The purpose herein is to awaken the UCLA Athletic Department to ponder the decisions being made that dramatically impact the lives of its former, current and future athletes. I am especially sensitive to the demonstrated insensitivity to African Americans which affects all racial groups. Is this but a tip of an iceberg?

UCLA Hall of Fame
Men's Basketball Inductees

1984
Kareem Abdul-Jabbar	'60s
Gail Goodrich	'60s
Walt Hazzard	'60s
Jackie Robinson	'40s
Bill Walton	'70s
Jamaal Wilkes	'70s
John Wooden	'40s - '70s

1985
George Stanich	'40s
Sidney Wicks	'70s

1986
Keith Erickson	'60s
Willie Naulls	'50s
Jerry Norman	'50s

1987
Don Barksdale	'40s
Dick Linthicum	'30s

1988
Sam Balter	'30s
Marques Johnson	'70s

1989
(none)

1990
Denny Crum	'50s
Mike Warren	'60s

1991
(none)

1992
Dave Mayers	'70s

1993
Bill Putnam	'70s
Curtis Rowe	'70s

1994
Don Bragg	'50s
Kiki Vandeweghe	'70s

1995
(none)

1996
(none

1997
David Greenwood	'70s
Frank Lubin	'30s

1998
Reggie Miller	'80s

1999
(none)

2000
Lucius Allen	'60s
Eddie Sheldrake	'50s

2001
Gary Cunningham	'60s
John Green	'60s

2002
Don MacLean	'90s

2003
Jerome "Pooh" Richardson	'80s

2004
Henry Bibby	'70s
Fred Slaughter	'60s

2005
Ed O'Bannon	'90s
Kenny Washington	'60s

Productive Proficiency
Willie Naulls' Objective Analysis of Bruin Dogs

Why the importance of the UCLA Dog Pound analysis? It has been over 30 years since John Wooden coached his last game, a 92-85 NCAA championship victory over the University of Kentucky on 31 March 1975. During his 27-year tenure at the helm of the UCLA Dog Pound, he developed 70% of UCLA's top-ten Career Proficiency Production leaders.

It is my contention that Proficient Production is highly correlated with mastery of fundamentals. Winning basketball games is determined by who scores the most points. Scoring is dramatically impacted by rebounding – regaining possession to give your team another opportunity to score and deny your opponents the same opportunity. The bottom line is that the team that scores the most points wins the game. Secondarily, the team which controls the backboards, more often than not, wins the game. Scoring and rebounding are the two vital categories which demonstrate individual contributions with the greatest influence on winning games.

Unfortunately, record-keeping has changed dramatically over the years, so statistical analyses from one generation to the next are difficult. Assists, turnovers and steals were not used to compute player effectiveness or productivity during my period of the Wooden era. In addition, the imposition of the mandatory freshmen season meant that many athletes' statistics included only three years of varsity play rather than four. It is important to note here that I believe that Coach Wooden continued in pursuing the development of his system of coaching basketball over the years and got better at doing his job. The zone press, reputed to have been developed by Coach's long time assistant Jerry Norman, was a weapon that his earlier players did not have. In addition, the wisdom in the early days of Coach Wooden's tenure was that strength training was inappropriate for basketball players. Indeed, NCAA rules prohibited athletes, including myself, from participating in organized games for the most part during the off-season.

The measure of Career Proficiency is accomplished herein by dividing each player's Career Scoring Average by two and adding that quotient to his Career Rebounding Average. During the 30 years since Coach Wooden retired, there have been an abundance of physically talented "dogs" who have amassed impressive statistics. Few, if any, have realized their full potential because they were not taught the basic fundamentals of sound basketball: balance, pivoting, defensive and offensive positioning, rebounding, boxing out, passing, proper shooting technique, defense, etc. These basics have to be taught by a qualified teacher. A true coach of basketball is called of God to teach the knowledge of its purpose through mastery of the game's fundamentals.

Determining the effectiveness of individual athletes during their times of glory in a given sport should be the goal. My sport was basketball. What follows is my suggestion for what could have been the matrix for use by founding leaders of the Hall of Fame to objectively and empirically honor those

The One and Only Great
Jackie Robinson

*returns to the House at UCLA in 1952
with his beloved wife, Rachel.
Greeted by Hall of Famer Bill Ackerman.*

*Jackie Robinson was the only four-sport
letterman in UCLA's history.
He competed in football, basketball
and track as well as baseball.*

*Some years later Jackie and I talked about
our common obstacles but I never shared
my appreciation and love for him.*

athletes who were most effective and productive during their playing days under Coach John Wooden and his successors. There are players whose names are included in my analysis who did not play under Coach, as noted. The significance is important in that coaching philosophies are different. Players' attitudes and demands for playing time changed dramatically at the end of the Wooden influence. Remember, Coach controlled the bones of playing time, not the players. It is rumored that some highly recruited players who played post-Wooden at UCLA demanded and were guaranteed bones as a condition for committing to our basketball program. I am not aware of one player during Coach's reign who was guaranteed playing time as a condition of coming to UCLA.

Statistical information courtesy of UCLA Sports Information

Willie Naulls' Objective Analysis of Bruin Dogs Career Most Productive Scorers

Rank	Name	# Games	Total Points	Career Avg.
1	**LEWIS ALCINDOR**			
	(KAREEM ABDUL-JABBAR)	**88**	**2325**	**26.42**
2	Don MacLean	127	2608	20.54
3	**BILL WALTON**	**87**	**1767**	**20.31**
4	**GAIL GOODRICH**	**89**	**1690**	**18.99**
5	Tracy Murray	98	1792	18.29
6	Reggie Miller	122	2095	17.17
7	Jason Kapono	127	2095	16.50
8	**WALT HAZZARD**			
	(MAHDI ABDUL-RAHMAN)	**87**	**1401**	**16.10**
9	**SIDNEY WICKS**	**90**	**1423**	**15.81**
10	**WILLIE NAULLS**	**79**	**1225**	**15.51**
11	Ed O'Bannon	117	1815	15.51
12	**WALT TORRENCE**	**77**	**1181**	**15.34**
13	**LUCIUS ALLEN**	**60**	**918**	**15.30**
14	**CURTIS ROWE**	**90**	**1371**	**15.23**
15	Kenny Fields	109	1638	15.03
16	**KEITH (JAMAAL) WILKES**	**90**	**1349**	**14.99**
17	David Greenwood	118	1721	14.58
18	**MARQUES JOHNSON**	**115**	**1659**	**14.43**
19	Charles O'Bannon	124	1784	14.39
20	**HENRY BIBBY**	**90**	**1293**	**14.37**
21	Toby Bailey	129	1846	14.31
22	Trevor Wilson	126	1798	14.27
23	**RICHARD WASHINGTON**	**87**	**1235**	**14.23**
24	J. R. Henderson	127	1801	14.18
25	**JOHN GREEN**	**81**	**1148**	**14.17**

"DOGS" who played for Coach Wooden in **BOLD CAPS**

Willie Naulls' Objective Analysis of Bruin Dogs
Career Most Productive Scorers

Rank	Name	# Games	Total Points	Career Avg.
26	JOHN VALLELY	58	799	13.78
27	MICHAEL WARREN	86	1176	13.67
28	Baron Davis	59	802	13.59
29	Shon Tarver	124	1575	12.70
30	Roy Hamilton	108	1355	12.55
31	JACK HIRSCH	59	736	12.47
32	EDGAR LACEY	62	758	12.23
33	Kiki Vandeweghe	113	1380	12.21
34	Tyus Edney	125	1515	12.12
35	Rod Foster	113	1365	12.08
36	Pooh Richardson	122	1461	11.98
37	Jerome Moiso	62	742	11.97
38	MORRIS TAFT	77	920	11.95
39	RON LIVINGSTON	48	572	11.92
40	DAVID MEYERS	89	1046	11.75
41	JaRon Rush	37	429	11.59
42	Kris Johnson	112	1294	11.55
43	GARY CUNNINGHAM	80	919	11.49
44	Earl Watson	129	1449	11.23
45	JOHN BERBERICH	52	582	11.19
46	JOHN MOORE	108	1202	11.13
47	Mike Sanders	109	1210	10.84
48	Dijon Thompson	89	942	10.58
49	Dan Gadzuric	122	1287	10.55
50	Jelani McCoy	78	814	10.44
51	STEVE PATTERSON	90	910	10.11
52	Darren Daye	114	1149	10.08

"DOGS" who played for Coach Wooden in **BOLD CAPS**

Willie Naulls' Objective Analysis of Bruin Dogs
Career Most Productive Scorers

Rank	Name	# Games	Total Points	Career Avg.
53	**KENNY WASHINGTON**	86	801	10.04
54	**DON JOHNSON**	61	596	9.77
55	**LYNN SHACKELFORD**	90	871	9.68
56	**KEITH ERICKSON**	87	834	9.59
57	**DON BRAGG**	108	1021	9.45
58	Darrick Martin	129	1195	9.26
59	T. J. Cummings	118	1062	9.00
60	**FRED SLAUGHTER**	87	768	8.83
61	Matt Barnes	121	1066	8.81
62	**BILL ELLIS**	52	446	8.58
63	Billy Knight	117	938	8.02
64	Mitchell Butler	130	1023	7.87
65	Gerald Madkins	123	937	7.62
66	Stuart Gray	78	585	7.50
67	**RALPH DROLLINGER**	86	625	7.27
68	George Zidek	104	742	7.13
69	**DOUG MCINTOSH**	85	543	6.39

"DOGS" who played for Coach Wooden in **BOLD CAPS**

Willie Naulls' Objective Analysis of Bruin Dogs Career Most Productive Rebounders

Rank	Name	# Games	Total Rebounds	Career Avg.
1	**BILL WALTON**	87	1370	15.75
2	**LEWIS ALCINDOR**			
	(KAREEM ABDUL-JABBAR)	88	1367	15.53
3	**WILLIE NAULLS**	79	900	11.39
4	**JOHN BERBERICH**	52	518	9.96
5	**SIDNEY WICKS**	90	894	9.93
6	**EDGAR LACEY**	62	569	9.18
7	**FRED SLAUGHTER**	87	791	9.09
8	**CURTIS ROWE**	90	796	8.84
9	David Greenwood	118	1022	8.66
10	**WALT TORRENCE**	77	653	8.48
11	**KEITH ERICKSON**	87	697	8.01
12	Trevor Wilson	126	1001	7.94
13	**STEVE PATTERSON**	90	706	7.84
14	Don MacLean	127	992	7.81
15	**MARQUES JOHNSON**	115	897	7.80
16	**JACK HIRSCH**	59	450	7.63
17	**KEITH (JAMAAL) WILKES**	90	663	7.37
18	Dan Gadzuric	122	896	7.34
19	Ed O'Bannon	117	820	7.01
20	**DON BRAGG**	108	751	6.95
21	JaRon Rush	37	256	6.92
22	Jerome Moiso	62	421	6.79
23	Jelani McCoy	78	528	6.77
24	**RICHARD WASHINGTON**	87	582	6.65
25	Stuart Gray	78	507	6.50

"DOGS" who played for Coach Wooden in **BOLD CAPS**

Willie Naulls' Objective Analysis of Bruin Dogs Career Most Productive Rebounders

Rank	Name	# Games	Total Rebounds	Career Avg.
26	J. R. Henderson	127	818	6.44
27	Charles O'Bannon	124	797	6.43
28	Tracy Murray	98	627	6.40
29	**RALPH DROLLINGER**	**86**	**546**	**6.35**
30	Kenny Fields	109	667	6.12
31	**JOHN MOORE**	**108**	**650**	**6.02**
32	**LUCIUS ALLEN**	**60**	**356**	**5.93**
33	**DAVID MEYERS**	**89**	**497**	**5.84**
34	**DOUG MCINTOSH**	**85**	**486**	**5.72**
35	**JOHN GREEN**	**81**	**457**	**5.64**
36	**DON JOHNSON**	**61**	**339**	**5.60**
37	**WALT HAZZARD** **(MAHDI ABDUL-RAHMAN)**	**87**	**475**	**5.46**
38	**KENNY WASHINGTON**	**86**	**463**	**5.38**
39	Mike Sanders	109	577	5.29
40	Toby Bailey	129	670	5.19
41	**GARY CUNNINGHAM**	**80**	**414**	**5.18**
42	Jason Kapono	127	647	5.09
43	Kiki Vandeweghe	113	569	5.04
44	**LYNN SHACKELFORD**	**90**	**449**	**4.99**
45	Matt Barnes	121	584	4.83
46	**BILL ELLIS**	**52**	**250**	**4.81**
47	**GAIL GOODRICH**	**89**	**415**	**4.66**
48	Pooh Richardson	122	565	4.63
49	T. J. Cummings	118	518	4.39
50	George Zidek	104	437	4.20

"DOGS" who played for Coach Wooden in **BOLD CAPS**

Willie Naulls' Objective Analysis of Bruin Dogs
Career Most Productive Rebounders

Rank	Name	# Games	Total Rebounds	Career Avg.
51	Reggie Miller	122	509	4.17
52	Mitchell Butler	130	539	4.15
53	**MORRIS TAFT**	**77**	**315**	**4.09**
54	**MICHAEL WARREN**	**86**	**341**	**3.97**
55	Darren Daye	114	452	3.96
56	Baron Davis	59	226	3.83
57	Shon Tarver	124	471	3.80
58	Earl Watson	129	484	3.75
59	Kris Johnson	112	410	3.66
60	Dijon Thompson	89	324	3.64
61	**HENRY BIBBY**	**90**	**316**	**3.51**
62	**JOHN VALLELY**	**58**	**202**	**3.48**
63	Tyus Edney	125	379	3.03
64	**RON LIVINGSTON**	**48**	**125**	**2.60**
65	Roy Hamilton	108	247	2.29
66	Gerald Madkins	123	269	2.19
67	Billy Knight	117	253	2.16
68	Darrick Martin	129	250	1.94
69	Rod Foster	113	191	1.69

"DOGS" who played for Coach Wooden in **BOLD CAPS**

Willie Naulls' Objective Analysis of Bruin Dogs Career Most Proficient Producers

Rank	Name	Career Avg. Score	Career Avg. Rebounds	Career Profi- ciency
1	**LEWIS ALCINDOR**			
	(KAREEM ABDUL-JABBAR)	**26.42**	**15.53**	**28.74**
2	**BILL WALTON**	**20.31**	**15.75**	**25.91**
3	**WILLIE NAULLS**	**15.51**	**11.39**	**19.15**
4	Don MacLean	20.54	7.81	18.08
5	**SIDNEY WICKS**	**15.81**	**9.93**	**17.84**
6	**CURTIS ROWE**	**15.23**	**8.84**	**16.46**
7	**WALT TORRENCE**	**15.34**	**8.48**	**16.15**
8	David Greenwood	14.58	8.66	15.95
9	**JOHN BERBERICH**	**11.19**	**9.96**	**15.56**
10	Tracy Murray	18.29	6.40	15.55
11	**EDGAR LACEY**	**12.23**	**9.18**	**15.29**
12	Trevor Wilson	14.27	7.94	15.08
13	**MARQUES JOHNSON**	**14.43**	**7.80**	**15.02**
14	**KEITH (JAMAAL) WILKES**	**14.99**	**7.37**	**14.87**
15	Ed O'Bannon	15.51	7.01	14.77
16	**GAIL GOODRICH**	**18.99**	**4.66**	**14.15**
17	**JACK HIRSCH**	**12.47**	**7.63**	**13.87**
18	**RICHARD WASHINGTON**	**14.23**	**6.65**	**13.77**
19	Kenny Fields	15.03	6.12	13.64
20	Charles O'Bannon	14.39	6.43	13.63
21	**LUCIUS ALLEN**	**15.30**	**5.93**	**13.58**
22	J. R. Henderson	14.18	6.44	13.53
23	**WALT HAZZARD**			
	(MAHDI ABDUL-RAHMAN)	**16.10**	**5.46**	**13.51**
24	**FRED SLAUGHTER**	**8.83**	**9.09**	**13.51**
25	Jason Kapono	16.50	5.09	13.34

"DOGS" who played for Coach Wooden in **BOLD CAPS**

Willie Naulls' Objective Analysis of Bruin Dogs
Career Most Proficient Producers

Rank	Name	Career Avg. Score	Career Avg. Rebounds	Career Profi-ciency
26	**STEVE PATTERSON**	**10.11**	**7.84**	**12.90**
27	**KEITH ERICKSON**	**9.59**	**8.01**	**12.81**
28	Jerome Moiso	11.97	6.79	12.77
29	Reggie Miller	17.17	4.17	12.76
30	**JOHN GREEN**	**14.17**	**5.64**	**12.73**
31	JaRon Rush	11.59	6.92	12.72
32	Dan Gadzuric	10.55	7.34	12.62
33	Toby Bailey	14.31	5.19	12.35
34	Jelani McCoy	10.44	6.77	11.99
35	**DAVID MEYERS**	**11.75**	**5.84**	**11.72**
36	**DON BRAGG**	**9.45**	**6.95**	**11.68**
37	**JOHN MOORE**	**11.13**	**6.02**	**11.59**
38	Kiki Vandeweghe	12.21	5.04	11.15
39	**GARY CUNNINGHAM**	**11.49**	**5.18**	**10.92**
40	Mike Sanders	10.84	5.29	10.84
41	**MICHAEL WARREN**	**13.67**	**3.97**	**10.81**
42	**HENRY BIBBY**	**14.37**	**3.51**	**10.70**
43	Pooh Richardson	11.98	4.63	10.62
44	Baron Davis	13.59	3.83	10.62
45	**DON JOHNSON**	**9.77**	**5.60**	**10.49**
46	**JOHN VALLELY**	**13.78**	**3.48**	**10.37**
47	Stuart Gray	7.50	6.50	10.25
48	**MORRIS TAFT**	**11.95**	**4.09**	**10.06**
49	**KENNY WASHINGTON**	**10.04**	**5.38**	**10.04**
50	Shon Tarver	12.70	3.80	10.15

"DOGS" who played for Coach Wooden in **BOLD CAPS**

Willie Naulls' Objective Analysis of Bruin Dogs
Career Most Proficient Producers

Rank	Name	Career Avg. Score	Career Avg. Rebounds	Career Proficiency
51	RALPH DROLLINGER	7.27	6.35	9.98
52	LYNN SHACKELFORD	9.68	4.99	9.83
53	Kris Johnson	11.55	3.66	9.44
54	Earl Watson	11.23	3.75	9.37
55	Matt Barnes	8.81	4.83	9.24
56	BILL ELLIS	8.58	4.81	9.10
57	Darren Daye	10.08	3.96	9.00
58	Tyus Edney	12.12	3.03	9.09
59	Dijon Thompson	10.58	3.64	8.93
60	DOUG MCINTOSH	6.39	5.72	8.91
61	T. J. Cummings	9.00	4.39	8.89
62	Roy Hamilton	12.55	2.29	8.57
63	RON LIVINGSTON	11.92	2.67	8.56
64	Mitchell Butler	7.87	4.15	8.08
65	George Zidek	7.13	4.20	7.77
66	Rod Foster	12.08	1.69	7.73
67	Darrick Martin	9.26	1.94	6.57
68	Billy Knight	8.02	2.16	6.17
69	Gerald Madkins	7.62	2.19	6.00

Proficiency is determined by dividing Career Scoring
Average by 2 and adding that number to Career
Rebounding Average to give equal weight to rebounding.

Career Proficiency =
Career Scoring Average/2 + Career Rebounding Average

"DOGS" who played for Coach Wooden in BOLD CAPS

Willie Naulls' Objective Analysis of Bruin Dogs
Individual Dogs' Best Season: Scoring

Season	Name	Total Points	Total Games	Avg. PPG	Rank
1968	**LEWIS ALCINDOR**				
	(KAREEM ABDUL-JABBAR)	**870**	**30**	**29.0**	**1**
1986	Reggie Miller	750	29	25.9	2
1965	**GAIL GOODRICH**	**744**	**30**	**24.8**	**3**
1956	**WILLIE NAULLS**	**661**	**28**	**23.6**	**4**
1990	Don MacLean	714	32	22.3	5
1959	**WALT TORRENCE**	**537**	**25**	**21.5**	**6**
1992	Tracy Murray	706	33	21.4	7
1971	**SIDNEY WICKS**	**638**	**30**	**21.3**	**8**
1972	**BILL WALTON**	**633**	**30**	**21.1**	**9**
1995	Ed O'Bannon	673	33	20.4	10
1976	**RICHARD WASHINGTON**	**644**	**32**	**20.1**	**11**
1978	David Greenwood	596	30	19.9	12
1977	**MARQUES JOHNSON**	**578**	**29**	**19.9**	**13**
1980	Kiki Vandeweghe	623	32	19.5	14
1962	**JOHN GREEN**	**559**	**29**	**19.3**	**15**
1998	J. R. Henderson	626	33	19.0	16
1964	**WALT HAZZARD**				
	(MAHDI ABDUL-RAHMAN)	**558**	**30**	**18.6**	**17**
1990	Trevor Wilson	570	31	18.4	18
1975	**DAVID MEYERS**	**566**	**31**	**18.3**	**19**
1983	Kenny Fields	523	29	18.0	20
1998	Toby Bailey	591	33	17.9	21
1997	Charles O'Bannon	565	32	17.7	22
1971	**CURTIS ROWE**	**525**	**30**	**17.5**	**23**
2001	Jason Kapono	551	32	17.2	24
1978	Roy Hamilton	481	28	17.2	25

"DOGS" who played for Coach Wooden in **BOLD CAPS**

Willie Naulls' Objective Analysis of Bruin Dogs
Individual Dogs' Best Season: Scoring

Season	Name	Total Points	Total Games	Avg. PPG	Rank
2004	Dijon Thompson	402	28	14.4	26
1993	Shon Tarver	550	33	16.7	27
1974	**KEITH WILKES**	**500**	**30**	**16.7**	**28**
1966	**MICHAEL WARREN**	**432**	**26**	**16.6**	**29**
1998	Kris Johnson	533	33	16.2	30
1972	**HENRY BIBBY**	**470**	**30**	**15.7**	**31**
1983	Darren Daye	456	29	15.7	32
1994	Tyus Edney	430	28	15.4	33
1981	Mike Sanders	417	27	15.4	34
1989	Pooh Richardson	470	31	15.2	35
2001	Earl Watson	471	32	14.7	36
1983	Rod Foster	410	29	14.1	37
2002	Matt Barnes	420	33	12.7	38
1953	**JOHN MOORE**	**315**	**25**	**12.6**	**39**
2001	Dan Gadzuric	375	32	11.7	40
1991	Darrick Martin	371	32	11.6	41
1954	**DON BRAGG**	**280**	**25**	**11.2**	**42**
2004	T. J. Cummings	307	28	11.0	43
1993	Mitchell Butler	305	33	9.2	44

"DOGS" who played for Coach Wooden in **BOLD CAPS**

Willie Naulls' Objective Analysis of Bruin Dogs
Individual Dogs' Best Season: Rebounding

Season	Name	Total Reb.	Total Games	Avg. RPG	Rank
1972	**BILL WALTON**	**506**	**30**	**16.9**	**1**
1968	**LEWIS ALCINDOR**				
	(KAREEM ABDUL-JABBAR)	**461**	**28**	**16.5**	**2**
1956	**WILLIE NAULLS**	**410**	**28**	**14.6**	**3**
1971	**SIDNEY WICKS**	**384**	**30**	**12.8**	**4**
1959	**WALT TORRENCE**	**289**	**25**	**11.6**	**5**
1978	David Greenwood	319	28	11.4	6
1961	**JOHN BERBERICH**	**296**	**26**	**11.4**	**7**
1977	**MARQUES JOHNSON**	**301**	**27**	**11.1**	**8**
1970	**STEVE PATTERSON**	**300**	**30**	**10.0**	**9**
1971	**CURTIS ROWE**	**299**	**30**	**10.0**	**10**
1965	**EDGAR LACEY**	**295**	**30**	**9.8**	**11**
1963	**FRED SLAUGHTER**	**281**	**29**	**9.7**	**12**
1988	Trevor Wilson	281	30	9.4	13
1964	**KEITH ERICKSON**	**272**	**30**	**9.1**	**14**
1994	Ed O'Bannon	245	28	8.8	15
1990	Don MacLean	287	33	8.7	16
1953	**DON BRAGG**	**217**	**25**	**8.7**	**17**
2001	Dan Gadzuric	275	32	8.6	18
1972	**KEITH (JAMAAL) WILKES**	**245**	**30**	**8.2**	**19**
1998	J. R. Henderson	259	33	7.8	20
1992	Tracy Murray	232	33	7.0	21
1953	**JOHN MOORE**	**174**	**25**	**7.0**	**22**
1997	Charles O'Bannon	221	32	6.9	23
1984	Kenny Fields	193	28	6.9	24
1991	Tracy Murray	213	32	6.7	25
1998	Toby Bailey	195	33	5.9	26
2001	Jason Kapono	183	32	5.7	27

"DOGS" who played for Coach Wooden in **BOLD CAPS**

Whine Time:
Retrospective on the
Black Skin Sacrifice

There are few things in life more debilitating to the cause of competitive expression than old folk complaining. Whining about how bad it was years ago can impede growth today – unless the **Lessons** inside the whine promote growth in every way. Be empathic. My unloading is the light that reveals the muzzled voice of a skin color's sacrifice.

A Racial Scar

What price harboring A Racial Scar
Like the jagged broken edge of a jar
pain in presence is never very far

Like a piercing poke
of being public brunt of a joke
in your heart to soak

Suppressed tears come and go
temporary relief – doesn't grow
festering and fermenting tumor does stow

Some resort to a Band-Aid's hope
in pills and ingested dope
Soon discover that's not the way to cope

Only through Belief in God the Son
is victory over racism conclusively won
and one's new life officially begun

So – when a piercing poke
reminds you of A Racial Scar
remember that Jesus died as Source to
    bear
the pain of the scab that a wicked word
    does tear

God's healing from inside – and
outward – to mature His desire
of redemption and righteousness
Christ in you – to inspire!

Thank you, Father, for Godly repentance
unto good works, my eternal sentence.

Amen

"Listen to learn. Speak only when spoken to. Control your anger and decisions." It was the committed mentality of her soul that drove my mother to body slam whoever came toward her children with an evil sham. Her attitude allowed me to develop from infancy, through my college years, behind and beyond the invisible spiritual wall of segregation. In the 1950s, the athletic world was ambivalent about Black athletes. Coaches only used Black players as a last move to directly impact wins or championships. Victories improved a coach's status and the potential financial rewards to his institution. Did my Coach, John Wooden, wish me well? Did he suspect that I was a time bomb ready to release the monster who was always speaking to me about the White man's intent?

It may sound like crying time of an introspective aging warrior, but who is to tell the other side of the story about how Black athletes dealt with the burden of not being a favorite son's color? There are many reasons that White players were on rosters of the teams that I integrated during my impacting years – those who made the cut and were included because of talent and those who were kept as the coach's personal preference. Black players rarely numbered more than three and they earned a position because they were more talented and kept their opinions unspoken.

In the coaching systems of the 1950s and '60s, collegiate and professional African American players were subjected to coaches who looked upon their skin color first – and last. Of an unspoken pressure mandate to be politically correct, coaches routinely asked themselves rhetorical questions. How many Black players should I recruit? How many can I politically have on the court at the same time? Where will they stay on campus? What do I do if we have an odd number to assign to rooms on the road? Should we spend the money for an extra room or do we decide which White player has the greatest tolerance of those folk? What will our fans and boosters think if the Black players attract the attention of White girls? Do we scare them up front with our hang-ups? Do we make an obvious example of a talented Black player who violates our unspoken and unwritten code for the behavior of

Black players – alone?

Any coach who entertained the above questions tip-toed near the line of covert racism. Some coaches openly practiced selection by color and were overtly racist. Racism stems from the notion that one's own ethnic stock is superior. Those coaches who claim that they were not racist but only conformed to the societal pressures established and enforced by the majority are ignoring the convictions in their hearts. Mom taught me that if you know something is polluted and you intentionally drink of its deeper waters to earn a check to feed your family, you become a part of the problem. Only through non-participation could you rid yourself of any blame or shame.

So what about Coach Wooden? Was he a racist? Did he contribute to the foundational structure of racism?

The number one basketball program in America in the 1950s was the University of Kentucky; thus the most highly regarded coaching reputation was that of its coach, Adolph Rupp. His opinion of mixing Black skinned athletes to play with and against White skinned athletes was well documented, which makes my point here. Before UCLA Basketball agreed to integrate Lexington, Kentucky, and its hotel, motion picture theater, transportation system and famed arena, Coach Wooden insisted on one thing: My team must stay together or we're not coming. I speculate that Coach Rupp and those in charge of guarding the gate which racism erects said, in effect, "OK, John, but you keep them Black boys in line, you hear?" Only God could have orchestrated this move. Coach Wooden was not the household name as we know him today. However, he lived my mother's mandate to me: to be quick to listen, slow to speak and slow to become angry. He opened doors with his quiet action. His demeanor allowed him to walk through the gates of racism without pouring gasoline on the fire of its fury.

Lesson: My mother taught me, "All things are possible with God. Prepare yourself, William! Be ready when God opens the gates of hell to dramatically express Himself in the devil's face. Don't forget my words of instruction. God will be God throughout eternity and the gates of hell will not prevail." Coach John R. Wooden was God's chosen agent to lead, as David did against the Philistines. In his heart, Coach knew: The Lord delivered David from the paw of the lion and the grasp of the bear. God will deliver me – and my army – to the battle scene and back to L.A.

So the victory was assured on God's bigger court of life. Faith to act on God's Word was the force that broke the dam which had held back hundreds of young Black athletes whose passion was basketball. Coach can say, *I did it God's Way*, which was the God given way to get it done in the '50s. Unquestionably, my adopted surrogate White skinned father was not a racist! Amen.

The fact that Coach Wooden recruited me indicates that even though he was raised in a racist society, he was wise enough not to let that hinder his search for any desirable and readily admissible, quality players. Some coaches were forced to that conclusion later to keep their teams competitive. After Sam Cunningham of the University of Southern California had wrecked Coach Bear Bryant's University of Alabama football team with a one man show, the coach is reputed to have called an emergency meeting, saying "You got to get me one of them . . . . !"

The best young basketball talent during my high school years was concentrated in African American high schools in east Los Angeles: Jefferson, Jordan and Polytechnic. Manual Arts and Fremont would emerge as athletic talent hot beds in the '60s and '70s. Jim Powell of Polytechnic was high school basketball Player of the Year during my sophomore year at San Pedro High School. (My cousin M. H. McGilvery should have at least shared the honor.) J. C. Gibson of Jefferson was Player of the Year during my junior year, and Jordan's Earl Battey and I shared the honor during my senior year. Gibson's teammates included Mack Taylor, Algin Sutton and Leo Hill, all of whom could and, I believe, would have eventually started at UCLA had they enrolled. Earl Battey's Jordan teammates included A. C. Lydge, Lee Potts, James Gamble, all of whom had talent equal or superior to that of my teammates at UCLA. Jim Powell of Poly was an enormous talent who could have dominated west coast basketball and should have had a career in the professional ranks.

Bill Johnson, my friend and first African American Captain of Los Angeles County Marshall's Department, speculated that most young Black athletes of the 1950s thought first about getting a job after high school. College sports were not promoted as attainable goals to most. Earl Battey, who committed to UCLA, opted for and became an All-Star in professional baseball, but the rest of the guys – I don't know. To my knowledge, only one other local college offered scholarships to any of the African American high school stars.

Larry Dugan and Bill Barnes went to Pepperdine University. UCLA and USC are the two major universities in town. By the mid 1950s, Coach had attracted Bobby Pounds from Bakersfield, California; Johnny Moore from Gary, Indiana; Morrie Taft from Polytechnic High School in Los Angeles; Dick "Skeets" Banton from Compton and myself from San Pedro. USC did not have African American athletes during my career at UCLA. Because of Coach's success many universities across the country would soon adopt Coach Bear Bryant's conviction: "You got to get me one of them . . . !"

God eventually removed evil's stranglehold and integrated USC Athletics. The university reaped the fruit of its decision by developing its first African American Heisman Trophy winner, Mike Garrett. He later led the Trojans to back-to-back NCAA Football Championships as Athletic Director in 2003 and 2004.

The most consistent similarity among Black college players was their superior talent and quiet behavior taught them by parents: to be quick to listen, slow to speak and, above all, slow to get angry. There were hundreds of more talented players who became casualties of negative response to African Americans who acted in the individual freedom that White boys flaunted. In those days of separate and unequal coverage of sports, coaches and the press had a way of describing athletes. White players were described as "giving 110% all the time." Coaches and sports writers who guarded the divide of White-affirmative-action described a gifted, fluent, self controlled African American athlete as sullen, "not wanting it badly enough," "having the ability to be as great as he wants to be," and "not coming to play every day." That same attitude displayed by White players led to their being described as "cool under pressure," "poker-faced," "introspective," "intelligent," or "independent thinker," "self-starter," "maverick" or "born leader." There are many more subtleties about the White world's reluctance to view athletes from a vantage point past their skin color or perceived cultural difference. The John Wooden model of a good public attitude was that, after a game, an observer wouldn't be able to tell whether a player's team had won or lost. Black athletes were criticized, as White athletes were glorified, for displaying the same behavior. The one "needed a fire lit under him." The other was "in control in all situations."

Three great players from the University of Nevada, Las Vegas – Johnson, Augmon and Anthony – when playing in the NCAA Final Four were described by one television announcer as "thugs" and "hoodlums," even as he characterized the Duke players and their coach as looking like "choir boys led by a priest." One of the athletes from UNLV was considered for the highest award given annually to collegiate basketball's outstanding player, the John Wooden Award. Was it possible for the Wooden Award board not to be biased based on the announcer's comments? Character assassination and the color card were covert no more. That same announcer from behind the black wall in his mind is still a nationally paid voice. His attitude about skin color has become less obvious to some. Today he accentuates the positive of White players while having little positive to say about Black players. God does have a sense of humor in that one of the young men that he labeled as a "hoodlum" is a highly respected television announcer receiving prime time exposure.

It is not wise to generalize about the character of individuals in a given profession, but in my experience with coaches from the 1940s through the 1960s, most were covertly racist. Coaches treated Black players differently. Even when one considers their practice of separating team members into different rooms or hotels or their bias about inter-racial dating or accepting Black players' exclusion from restaurants or their attitudes in voting for All-Stars or All-America Teams, Race and Color of Skin were used by those leaders in a world where young men of all races laid their performance and passions on the line, to be evaluated justly in open competition. Not one White coach that I knew of spoke up and said that Black players had feelings, that they hurt when injustice was imposed on them.

Few will remember that a player from Santa Clara was voted MVP in Northern California over Bill Russell of the NCAA Championship University of San Francisco Dons in his junior year. Russ took it as a sucker punch in the gut, but what about the guy Northern California honored to exalt a skin color? Black players were treated like tolerated minorities, to be tokened into the White world for only as long as they had talent and physical strength to exploit. They were hooked up to their entre-preneurs' wagons to pull them, in mule fashion, toward the victorious finish lines for their profit, gain and fame. When a Black player couldn't do it any more, because of his lameness of state, he was professionally shot and discarded as an undesirable liability. I believe that none before Bill Russell would coach or be hired in administration. Of course, one might say that was life then for everyone. Is it that simple?

Most coaches looked at me through the filtered eyes of a racially separated upbringing. Coach Wooden gave chosen Black athletes an equal chance to play for his team, and our country should be grateful and honor him for his pioneering decisions.

My appeal is to delve into your most empathic self, to put yourself into the position of every Black athlete of the 1950s or 1960s who had talent enough to deserve a scholarship to play sports in college and was tokened into institutions – especially state universities supported by taxpayers of all races such as UCLA, Ohio State, Michigan State, Florida, etc. Begin to sense the humiliation at every level of competition for us, witnessing less talented players being used ahead of and instead of us – and being honored because they were promoted by their coaches, who allowed them to play through the learning curve. Those White players were given the benefit of the doubt as 110% effort guys, even as the reputation of the coach's Black players was devalued by remarks to the press, that "he could be as good as he wants to be" or "he could be great if he wanted it badly enough" or "he needs a fire lit under him to move." What insulting labels! They could and would be used later as character flaw reasons to deny African Americans opportunities for employment in the athletic, corporate and business worlds. One of the new descriptions of African Americans used by racists who are asked for recommendations regarding employment is, "She is not a self-starter."

During one high school seven-inning baseball

game I pitched and won, I hit two home runs and struck out 12 players. The reporter commented in his column the next day that I had been "an in-and-out performer all year." That meant inconsistent. Later on in the same article he stated that my ERA was about one run per game. He did not mention that my strikeout average was 12 per seven-inning game and my batting average was over .500. I hadn't lost a game and I was first string All-City at year's end. "In and out performer" were words used by this writer to brainwash his readers into devaluing my consistent and dependable performance.

Another incident from the '50s involved the annual All-America game of that era which pitted current year All-Americans against the New York Knicks at Madison Square Garden in New York City. The coach of the All-Americans was a guy named Tom Blackburn who coached the University of Dayton. We warmed up before the game which was staged after we had a few days to practice together. I came back to the bench, took off my warm-ups and prepared to start the game as I had practiced with the first team the previous days. Coach Blackburn abruptly said that Dave Piontek was starting ahead of me. After two minutes or so into the game, he called my name and said, with his very thick southern drawl, "I don't know what I was thinking, Willie. I should have started you. You are the All-American people paid to see." So I entered the game as a sub.

The reaction after the game from the reporters was, "Willie, why didn't you start? Did you break the team rules or something?" The burn inside me wanting to scream "Ask that racist pig over there" subsided as I stared into their non-compassionate faces in this contrived situation. Glancing for the final time at the authority who had again used me, I was as a ghost in silence – and passed yet another opportunity to pour gasoline on the flame of situational racism.

I wanted Coach Wooden to say something, anything, on my behalf.

African American players at UCLA were not promoted in my day to get national post-season recognition and awards. I remember Coach Wooden publicly lauding an accomplished player from the east coast, Tom Gola, as being the finest all around player he had ever seen, before and during my sophomore season. He was an effective, competitive White player, on everyone's All-America first team. Because of his lack of speed and average jumping ability, he would have been just another good player in the open competition of ghetto games in parks around the country. At the end of my senior year, Coach said the same things about me. The difference? His lack of comments about my talent before and during the year, before season's end, had a huge impact on the recognition that I did not receive, thus directly influencing my perceived value to pro teams. I understand that it was not his job to promote my athletic career, but he certainly did help to promote Tom Gola's.

Perception is directly influenced by respected voices, and Coach's evaluations impacted public opinion in the college basketball world. He thought it was appropriate to give honor to a player from another team, but not to his players at UCLA. His philosophy was that honor should go to his team and not to any one individual on his team. When he retired as coach, everything changed and the new thinkers voted to retire great players' jerseys – something Coach publicly stated he would never allow. Asked about not retiring my jersey, #33, he had said, "Willie is the greatest all around player I have ever coached; he's the greatest I've ever seen . . . a better all around player than the great Bill Russell." If I were a White player, would UCLA have two #33 jerseys retired? 33A, Willie Naulls, and 33B, Lew Alcindor/Kareem Abdul-Jabbar?

Coach Wooden had minimum good to say about me while I was an active player at UCLA. The exception above was an out of character outburst after the last regular season game of my senior year before the NCAA playoffs included in an article written by the beloved Sam Balter in which Coach is quoted.

In the early days of this twenty-first century, Coach Wooden again pushed my sensitivity button. From 1998 to 2004 my wife and I owned a home in Gainesville, Florida. Malaika, our youngest child, had decided to attend University of Florida located there, where she participated on the Gators volley-ball team during two Final-Four seasons. Dr. Charles E. Young, the former Chancellor of UCLA for many years, became the President of the University of Florida during our stay in Gainesville. During one of my appointments with Dr. Young we discussed a fundraising event that University of Florida Basketball Coach Billy Donovan and I staged. The last thing on my agenda was to intro-duce the idea of Coach Wooden coming to speak at the University. The University's Athletic Director, Jeremy Foley, many administrators, coaches and

One for the Book

by Sam Balter

Bruins Still Subdued After Spectacular Year

There was not the hilarity you would have imagined in the UCLA dressing-quarters following Saturday night's smashing 97-84 victory over the Bruins' crosstown rivals, Southern California.

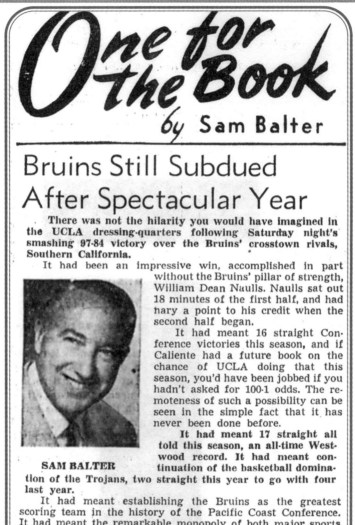

SAM BALTER

It had been an impressive win, accomplished in part without the Bruins' pillar of strength, William Dean Naulls. Naulls sat out 18 minutes of the first half, and had nary a point to his credit when the second half began.

It had meant 16 straight Conference victories this season, and if Caliente had a future book on the chance of UCLA doing that this season, you'd have been jobbed if you hadn't asked for 100-1 odds. The remoteness of such a possibility can be seen in the simple fact that it has never been done before.

It had meant 17 straight all told this season, an all-time Westwood record. It had meant continuation of the basketball domination of the Trojans, two straight this year to go with four last year.

It had meant establishing the Bruins as the greatest scoring team in the history of the Pacific Coast Conference. It had meant the remarkable monopoly of both major sports of the college year in the Conference, the basketball sweep adding on to an undefeated Conference football season.

It had meant individual scoring records for the Menace of Venice, the irrepressible Naulls, who came back in the second half to score 22 points in that period alone. It had meant the Conference championship in shooting accuracy for guard Morry Taft, and the highest scoring total in Conference history by a guard for the protagonist of the nation's most spectacular jump shot.

It had meant a great career finish for Alan Herring, too, along with Naulls and Taft. Herring had turned in another of his steady, valued performances, to earn for himself the dubious title of 'Most Underrated Man in the League.'

It had meant a shot at the national championship, a reminder of which came from a gracious Trojan rooting section, which cheered the Bruins as they left the floor with a yell of "Beat San Francisco."

*   *   *

The Moment Was Ripe

It was unquestionably a moment for celebration.

Yet these Bruins doffed their togs quietly, took their showers, and sucked on quartered oranges in pensive mood. Even after the great triumphs of the immediate past, the future was with them more.

An unlucky geographical happenstance had matched them in the very first round of NCAA play with the one team in the nation which was considered unbeatable, which, over two years, had won 51 straight games, and which was the defending champion of the United States.

Only jaunty Carroll Adams referred to the triumph that had just taken place. He stopped to shake hands with Coach Wooden and say briefly, "Well, coach, we made it number sixteen." (Adams has another year of eligibility, but he can graduate in June, and since he is a family man with responsibilities, plans to do so.)

Wooden seemed lost in thought, too. He said, "Yes, thanks," to Adams' comment, a rather bare acknowledgement.

Then Naulls passed by from his shower, a glistening study of heroic proportions in nude bronze (such as Odusseus never was) and Wooden was snapped back into the present.

A man not given to superlatives, Wooden said to me: "He is the greatest I have ever coached. He is the greatest I have ever seen. And you know I have seen many.

"Perhaps, over a full career, there have been some greater. But, in a single-season play, none. Who else can do all the varied things he can do, and does, game after game? Not Freeman. Not Russell. (The unexpressed thought: was it fair to be less skillful, as Russell is, but more demoralizing and frightening because of that great attribute of boarding-over the defensive basket, at which Russell has no peer?) Willie is amazing, just amazing."

*   *   *

Future Is With Them

The undefeated champions were still subdued as they left for the bus.

Their coach had a fetish on the subject. He had told them often: "Win or lose, I want you to leave the dressing-room after a game with head high, chins up. I don't want anyone to be able to tell, just by looking at you, whether you won or lost."

Somewhere in literature a man with poetic turn had once written, "Treat those two Imposters, Victory and Defeat, alike, and you'll be the better for it."

It was not easy advice to follow this Saturday night in the locker-rooms of a beach-city high school, for the occasion was ripe for celebration. But a tempering influence hung over the gym to make the subdued quiet understandable: the influence of the immediate future that lay waiting in the small college town of Corvallis, Oregon.

professors openly lauded Coach's wisdom. Dr. Young thought it a great idea and requested of me that I speak to Coach on his behalf.

When Anne and I returned to California, I initiated an appointment with Coach to discuss including the University of Florida on his speaking calendar. After Coach agreed to come to Florida, we concluded that it would be of greater benefit to the students and general public in Gainesville if Coach were to speak to the entire community and to do it on the campus of the University of Florida. Dr. Young asked me what I thought a reasonable fee would be for Coach Wooden. I suggested that Coach Wooden be compensated somewhere between the amount reportedly paid to former Soviet President Gorbachev and that paid to Coach Bob Knight. He agreed to take my recommendation under advisement with the other appropriate entities, thanked me for my input and stated that he would handle it from there.

Upon his arrival in Gainesville, Coach was received as the Pope of Athletics. Anne and I saw him during his three-day stay when we were invited to a dinner in his honor at the home of President and Mrs. Young and again prior to his speaking engagement in the University's Center for Performing Arts. Coach prayed over our meal. A dear friend from our Bible study group stated that he felt uncomfortable asking me how I felt about Coach Wooden's not mentioning my name publicly during his three days of public sharing in Gainesville. He uncovered my vulnerability to desire the approval of Coach Wooden, my self-appointed surrogate father. I admitted that my old crusted wounds had been somewhat reopened, as

THE WHALE—Willie Naulls, UCLA center who leads PCC in scoring and rebounds, is rated by Coach John Wooden best all-around cager in Bruin history.

Los Angeles Times, 1 March 1956

HIS GREATEST PLAYER

Wooden Rates Naulls Better All-Around Cager Than Russell

Coach never thanked Anne and me for introducing, negotiating and promoting his being paid handsomely to share with the Gainesville community. I didn't respect in myself the uneasiness I felt when Coach talked about his "boys" without mentioning my name. Of course one could conclude that, in his wisdom, he determined not to say anything because he had nothing good to say about me.

In his defense, he may never have been told of my role in the events which brought him to Gainesville. I have always wanted him to know that I am one of his DOGS who has come as far as any of the others from where we individually started. I am ashamed that I resented that he has never publicly acknowledged, to my knowledge, that some of us, his players, came from deep racial socioeconomic oppression and have come further personally – to forgive – than those few post-1960 superstar players to whom he gives humorous lip service for public adoration. Anne and I prayed together for forgiveness of our selfish agreement that Coach's words were self-promoting and not team edifying. We prayed that his intent was approved of God.

Expression of my inner truth will invoke protective responses from those who are prone to defend segregated history and not turn the light on the ongoing myths of segregated reputation. Character, as taught by my mom and Coach, is what a person thinks to say and then to do. I can never influence the character of Coach. He controls his character, not I. My remarks are not about character because Coach John Wooden is a man of Godly character. I'm speaking as a son does about his surrogate father whose approval he always sought.

We can now better understand Scripture which

says, "The heart is deceitful above all things and beyond cure. Who can understand it?" (Jeremiah 17:9). The word "deceitful" is the funnel through which all kinds of things happen that we allow to happen, without a word of protest, even though an entire race or skin coloring is being unfairly discriminated against. That drum has been beaten for years and its *thump thump* is drowned out by the loud voice of inclusiveness and an adjustable scale of standards of entry.

Baring my soul relieves me to begin the next of my life's journeys without the weight of tact. Remember the line from *The Godfather*, voicing that "niggers" ain't nothing but "animals." Tact in my days was an attitude of Whites to "sweep under the carpet" any criticism of the insensitive acts of coaches toward Black skinned players, for they were "nothing but animals." "Blessed is the man who does not condemn himself by what he approves" (Romans 14:22b). God has said, and I share His Word on this subject, "When you stand praying, if you have anything against anyone, forgive him, so that your Father in heaven may forgive you your sins" (Mark 11:25). I know God hates pride and forgives all of us when we earnestly repent of what we know to be wrong.

I must always remember to widen my scope, which self pity narrows. I have stopped thinking of Coach Wooden as the man who didn't want to be my surrogate father. He will tell you he has faults just as I have. It is God who is to be glorified for giving Coach Wooden and me loving parents and wives and family and long days upon this earth lived in prosperity of spirit, soul and body. And God is to be given the glory in everything we think, say and do that produces good fruit for our families' benefit, and good fruit in abundance to share with others God puts in our paths.

Lesson: "You shall have no other gods before Me," says the Lord God Almighty (Exodus 20:3).

In the final analysis, some may think it presumptuous of me, a victim of situational ethics of a coach or an athletic institution, to speak up and that I should just shut up and not un-scab an old sore's deeply rooted wound. They may be right in their opinion. I speak for all the other Black "dogs" with similar stories. Sweeping us under the carpet promotes dust from which future generations could ingest a Dog Pound virus. Only through public Godly repentance toward forgetting can all DOGS be healed. The purpose of sharing my heart is to cause people to think. "Pray for all those who are insensitive to you and want you to remain whomever they, through your skin color, think you should be." Mom's eternal words of wisdom are timeless **Lessons**.

I am Coach John R. Wooden's first of three All-Americans to average a double-double over his UCLA career (the others being Lewis Alcindor and Bill Walton) and first four-year NBA All-Star and three-time NBA World Champion. He said at the end of my senior season at UCLA, "Willie is the best I have ever coached – the best I have ever seen." We had just won *sixteen straight* games to go undefeated in conference play, a record which still stands after the 2004-2005 season. In the recent television interview with Barry LeBrock, Coach restated that I was his best ever all around player in his post offense.

It is difficult writing about Coach using what might be considered less than reputation-enhancing words. Knowing that I can potentially damage only my own reputation in the minds of some through my honesty, it is encouraging to know that many people will know the intent of my words' impact.

Coaches' Reapers

Deep within the hearts of coaches do
    dwell
stories in truth they are yet to tell.
God and they are left as the Keepers
of their secret thoughts about all us
    Reapers!

In the fall of 1994, it had been 42 years since I had decided to align myself under the authority and influence of Coach Wooden. During those many years he never specifically indicated to me that he thought of me in any other realm than as one of his Dogs. Coach responded to an invitation to add his thoughts to those of others on the occasion of my 60th birthday. The following note was sent to Anne who included it in one of the eleven books she amassed and gave to me at a surprise birthday party.

All these years I never knew. Maybe I should have known. Love is an action, not a word. Coach Wooden had been acting as though he loved me throughout the many years of our association. His silence of verbal expression about his inner grace toward me had blinded my open-mindedness on the subject. At the moment I read his words a cloud of insecurity was scattered away by the motions of the Power in Love.

Oct. 8, 1994

Dear Willie,

Your accomplishments as a high school, college and professional athlete and your achievements in the business world were all truly outstanding, but your turning to full time service for our Lord surpasses all.

I was blessed to have had the opportunity to work with you during your collegiate days, was happy to see your success as a professional athlete and business man, but am more proud of your devotion to your family and your decision to enter the ministry where you will have the privilege of helping many others find the Gateway to Heaven.

I love you, Willie, for what you are.

With great affection for you and yours,
Coach Wooden

Coach Wooden's Birthday Note

Thank you, Willie Naulls, for your love and concern
John Wooden
I Cor 13

Coach Wooden

"Whoever would love life and see good days
must keep his tongue from evil
and his lips from deceitful speech."
I Peter 3:10

For LOVE IS!

From Pyramid of Success to Pyramid of Promise – by Faith

Is He Is or Is He Ain't – a Saint?

I've been asked countless times over the
    years:
Is Coach Wooden a believer?
Or just a modest country boy
    overachiever?
Coach's Pyramid of Success Devotional
    is out
Now all Christian doubters can shout
JOHN ROBERT WOODEN is a Believer!
    and
Christ through him is the Achiever.

Many years ago, after retiring from professional
basketball, I picked up the last of the three Boston
Celtics championship rings I had earned and headed
home to Los Angeles. Ten years had passed since I
left UCLA to begin my NBA career with the Hawks.
I called Coach Wooden and asked him for an
audience. He agreed and I again found myself
sitting across from him at his desk, scanning his
walls filled with photos of past UCLA players and
teams. His Pyramid of Success was prominent and
prompted me to ask him a question I had long
entertained. Pointing, I asked, "Do you use the
word 'faith' at the top of your Pyramid to mean the
Faith of God?" He said that was not what he had in

mind, but more in line with his concern that his pupils/players develop personal faith in themselves.

As I sensed his uneasiness, I recalled Mom's teaching on judging others: "Look in the mirror!" My mom's words had the same effect as Coach's in that her words caused me to stop and think. Mom's one-liner was, "There are twenty-four hours in a day for you to mind your own business and twenty-four hours for you to leave other folks' alone." Today I know that the question of types of faith is most important because without the God kind of Faith, it is impossible to please God.

Coach Wooden taught me for a length of time that was second only to that of my mother. I mention that to give insight into my license to sense his uneasiness. Once before in a similar setting I asked his opinion about a decision I had made during a closely contested UCLA game against Stanford in Palo Alto during my senior year. Morrie Taft, my teammate, drove to the basket and shot as he was fouled. He missed the shot and I jumped and tipped the ball into the basket. Both officials at that split second were turned and looking away from the play and did not see me touch the ball. When they turned back toward the point of action, the ball was coming down through the net. Both called the shot good and Morrie was happy, standing at the free-throw line to attempt the completion of his three-point-play. There was a near riot among the Stanford coaches, players and fans who had seen what both officials had missed, that I had tipped the ball into the basket. The basket should not have counted. After about five minutes of violent reaction and debate, George Selleck,

George Selleck

Stanford University Guard

A worthy foe

*All-Coast Conference guard and
fierce competitor.
George became an ordained minister,
motivational speaker and author*

Stanford's All-Coast star player, came over to me as I sat on the court behind the basket and said, "Willie, you know you tipped the ball in, didn't you?" I looked at him and my mother said through me, "Yes, I tipped it in."

He jumped up, ran across the court, grabbed both referees and brought them over. I was looking around at the crowd and then into the eyes of the head official. He asked, "Willie, did you tip the ball in?"

"Yes, sir, I did." Mom was right there to tell the truth.

He thanked me for my honesty, went over to the scorer's table, cancelled the two points that Morrie and our team had been credited with and gave him two free throws. The game continued and we won, in overtime as I recall. George Selleck became a good friend and an ordained pastor. After graduation from Stanford, he sometimes used this story in his sermons.

Some years later in one of our therapy sessions, I asked Coach whether I had made the right decision. There was uneasiness to field a question to determine where he stood on an issue. He said, "Well, Willie, an individual has to make up his own mind in a situation like that. There are your teammates and the team to consider, not just yourself. But a man has to make up his own mind in a situation that affects so many others."

It is difficult to know how he felt really and I don't care to speculate on what he would think if we had lost the game. One could deduce from his remarks that a man is influenced by what he has been taught. A man must decide who he chooses to be by the decisions he alone makes or approves. I made a decision that directly affected his team and I asked Coach for his approval of my decision. His evaluation of my decision was that it was up to me entirely. I was his captain and he trusted my judgment to do whatever made me comfortable. My mom's voice was not so open-minded as God gave me the peace to tell the truth even when she was miles away. I have concluded that my mentor, Coach Wooden, would have made the same choice I did.

Another question often asked of me is my opinion about Coach Wooden's much publicized position on God and family. Even when I declare that I'm not the Bible answer man on my coach, those ministers and scholars insist on hearing my thoughts about what they have read about Coach. So, here I go again.

Coach is quoted as saying that his priority of thought and action always placed his wife and family first. I deduced that he isn't describing a competition of loyalty between his family and God. He generally adds that he is certain "the Master understands." My mom taught me the Biblical mandate that God demands that we publicly declare Him Number One and "have no other gods" before Him. As Coach surmises, his character and reputation plead God's under-standing. I herein confess that most of my life God was not Number One and neither was my family. Occupying that lofty position were "lust of the eyes, lust of the flesh and the pride of life." My biggest challenge since I committed my life to the ministry of Jesus Christ has been being judgmental. God is the final judge of each of us through His Word.

Matthew Henry's Commentary on the Whole Bible

speaks with clarity on the priority of our choices. If we "observe that which [God commands]" of us, "we cannot expect the benefit of the promises unless we make conscience of the precepts." In other words, one's conscience must be in line with Biblical teaching. One such precept is stated in Exodus 34:14: "Do not worship any other god, for the Lord, whose name is Jealous, is a jealous God." That is, one must not give divine honor to any creature, and for good reason: It is at one's own peril, as God is "as tender in the matter of His worship as a husband is of the honour of the marriage-bed. Jealousy is called 'the rage of a man' (Proverbs 6:34, KJV), but [Jealousy] is God's holy and just displeasure. Those cannot worship God aright who do not worship Him alone." (*Matthew Henry's Commentary on the Whole Bible, Volume I,* p. 336)

A good teacher inspires thought and pursuit of understanding. Later on in our relationship, I pondered Coach's answer to my question about the "faith" in his Pyramid. Again, his answer caused me to pursue the deeper spiritual meaning of the word *faith*, which eluded me until I committed my life to serving in the ministry of Jesus Christ. A personal relationship with Christ Jesus is the only way to know what real Faith is. In Scripture we are told that without Faith it is impossible to please God (Hebrews 11:6). His Word gives us the universal truth about Faith in the context of Paul's illumination to believers regarding Jewish food customs:

> *So whatever you believe about these things [choice of eating habits] keep between yourself and God. Blessed is the man who does not condemn himself by what he approves. But the man who has doubts is*

*condemned if he eats, because his eating is not from Faith; and **everything that does not come from Faith is sin.*** *Romans 14:22-23 (emphasis mine)*

One's faith is a private personal choice, as demonstrated in the life of Coach Wooden.

Coach Wooden's perspective about life's issues outside of basketball was rarely revealed in his answers to my specific questions. He was not the spiritual pharmacy where I could get a prescription filled to anesthetize my soul with God's healing balm. So our relationship remains in the shallowness of Dog Trainer to Dog with no truth in sincerity to the other. By truth in sincerity I mean the same depth of respect from him toward me that he gives to his family, the same Spirit of Godly respect that I have always given him. I expect that my telephone calls will be returned in the same zeal of respect as Coach gives publishers or the President of the United States. I am one of his Bruin Dogs and I will keep trying to get another audience with Coach before this book is published.

As my coach and wise counselor, Coach Wooden fulfilled his responsibility to inspire me to think. On the subject of faith, I was allowed to make up my mind without the intrusion of his spiritual conviction about God. I was raised to know specifically that I needed the God kind of Faith to survive in a world which looked upon me as a skin color – an adjective, and not a unique noun before God. Parents have the mandate to "train up their children in the Way they should go" (Proverbs 22:6). Having "the God kind of Faith" (Mark 11:22) is a virtue that I choose to live daily. Coach Wooden encouraged me to develop strong faith in myself even as he lived the God kind of Faith before me. He and my mom were role models to be emulated.

Coach John Wooden of Westwood
A Messenger On Call

Coach John Wooden of Westwood has a
    message for all
Industriousness and **enthusiasm**, the
    cornerstones of his call
Focused on **friendship** and **loyalty**, he
    stresses **cooperation**
and mastery of **intentness** of **initiative**
    through **self controlled** participation
Not to forget **alertness** and **condition** in
    developing **team spirit's skill**
of maturing **competitive greatness, poise**
    and **confidence** to fulfill
Inspired by **sincerity** of **ambition**, and an
    honest desire to be **"as He,"**
men and women can achieve their best
    through responsible **adaptability**
Reliability on the **resourcefulness**
    possessed in **integrity**'s might
is the victory of the good **fight** of **faith**,
    through **patience**'s insight
So, the message of life, of Coach
    Wooden's call –
SUCCESS is a reward to anyone who
    gives his or her all

Through barking, howling and whining, this Bruin Dog of the Coach John Wooden Pound has unpacked all his inner store of harbored fouls, especially those of the flagrant and intentional, mean spirited variety.

Early in the summer following my senior year I was drafted by the Professional NBA Hawks. After the disappointment of not making the Olympic team, I was honored by the NCAA Championship team, the University of San Francisco Dons, who chose me to play with them on a two-month State Department-sponsored tour of Central and South America. The next volume of *Levitation's View: Lessons Voiced from an Extraordinary Journey* will chronicle my stepping out of the world of Coach Wooden's UCLA Basketball program into the professional basketball ranks. I was twenty-one years old and ready to explore the world.

Volume III: The World Years will be available in 2006.

*Willie,
Bill Russell,
K. C. Jones and the
NCAA Champion
University of San
Francisco Dons
Basketball Team
arrive in Guatemala*

16 June 1956

*Fulfilling my dreams
from 7th grade, we
toured and were
undefeated throughout
Central and South
America, sponsored by
the U. S. State
Department.*

TRES DE LOS FAMOSOS BASKETBOLISTAS "DONS" EN LIMA

llegaron a esta Capital los famosos basket bolistas "Dons" de la Universidad de San Francisco, que están efectuando una jira por Cen tro y Sudamérica. Aquí en Lima, se presentarán 4 de agosto en el Estadio Nacional.— La vis ta presenta a tres de los mejores jugadores y de color, al centro el mejor basketbolista yan qui William Russel, que mide 2m. 05 a su izquierd Naulls, otro gigante de 1m. 95 y a su derecha K. C. Jones, que junto con Russel forman par del team olímpico de basketbol de los Estados Unidos para Melbourne.

**garon anoche los basketbolista
ons" de la "U" de San Francisc**

*Willie and the University of San Francisco Dons
Basketball Team arrive in Lima, Peru,
during a State Department-sponsored tour
of Central and South America.*

*The Dons, who were back-to-back NCAA
Champions for the 1954-55 and 1955-56 seasons,
invited Willie to join them on this tour as he
was voted their most outstanding competitor.*

*Pictured in their California cool hats are
K. C. Jones • Bill Russell • Willie Naulls*

When You Cry, You Cry Alone?

Somehow my soul never quite grew
    beyond
as unknowingly I embraced the devil's
    con
and through my father's hostile rejection
    of me
it caused my heart to cower – my soul
    yearning to be free
Whenever do we take the time to think
as the doing of life flashes in the blur of a
    blink
stammering – who am I and how can I
    protect myself to survive
outside the best nest of the – people
    needing people –– contrive?
In the worst of times – when the razor's
    edge cut so deep
I cried out of tears – alone – no one could
    hear me weep
Nobody looked deep enough to ask,
    "How you feeling inside?"
Stud in appearance caused
    communication to glide
Weaving in between – I never quite got
    a fix
in the mortar of living – just past in
    betwixt
Everybody thought, He can handle it,
    which ostensibly I did
as the shallowness inside relationships
    continuously slid

Then one day amid a mid morning's
    surprise
LOVE's intervention awakened my
    dormant spiritual eyes
thawing the cell block of self protection
    retrofitted in me
the Truth foundation promised emerged
    and set me free
In the best of times – now – the tears of
    joy overflowing
out of the abundance of Christ's Life's
    Seed sowing
exposed the Crying Alone agenda as a
    promotion of lies
because joy is His promise to the one
    who on Him relies